THE DARK KNIGHT RETURNS

BATMAN

THE DARK KNIGHT
RETURNS

FRANK MILLER

with KLAUS JANSON and LYNN VARLEY
Lettered by JOHN COSTANZA
Batman created by BOB KANE

BATMAN: THE DARK KNIGHT RETURNS
ISBN: 1 85286 798 1
ISBN-13: 9781852867980

Published by Titan Books, a division of Titan Publishing Group Ltd., 144 Southwark Street, London SE1 0UP.

Printed in Spain. This edition first published: May 1997.
20 19 18 17

Cover Illustration by Frank Miller, Klaus Janson and Lynn Varley.

Table of Contents

There's this little saloon you'll find up and running and packed with patrons before most of us are ready for our morning coffee.

The joint's two subway levels beneath the streets of downtown Metropolis.

Step out at the Schuster stop on the southbound side, take two lefts, walk maybe fifteen feet and you're right on top of it.

But you could just as easily walk right past it and never know it was there.

There's no sign up. Not even a door. Just a dark hallway that looks like a good place for a murder.

Take a breath. Follow the cigarette stink and the bluesy jukebox sounds inside.

It's a tolerable little gin mill. Get there before the morning rush, and you're likely to find a stool.

Your first clue that there's something wrong about the place is the bartender. You'll never forget his face. He's a hulk of a guy who's seen way too much. A broken man with laser-red eyes. His forehead's a fractured cantilever, an avalanche waiting to happen. His skin's gone a little gray from its natural chartreuse.

He's got a voice like Coke bottles getting ground up under a door.

His name is Jones.

He says he's from Mars.

And nobody tells him he's nuts, not one of these sad old barflies. It's not that they're scared of him, either.

They've seen and done things that are supposed to be impossible.

They're not the kind to out-and-out brag about being able to bench-press cars or run faster than a speeding bullet or jump up into the air and stay there. Nah. Not these guys.

These guys, they've got nothing to prove. Been there. Done that.

Except for old "Snapper" always at the same stool at the end, living up to his nickname, snapping his fingers in time to the music and rattling on and on and on about mighty powers, globe-spanning

TRUTH TO POWER

JAMES OLSEN

continued

continued from page 21

adventures, nefarious world conquerors, you name it.

He never stops snapping his damn fingers. And he never stops sucking back the sauce and jabbering about the old days. The glory days.

The "Golden Age" he calls it.

The age of heroes.

And all the other old farts, they grunt and nod and grumble at each other, swapping old jokes they've swapped a thousand times. Even fat, beet-red old "Penguin" chirps out a curse or two before bursting into tears.

Then they get talking. And if you've got half a brain, you listen.

They talk about amazing adventures, sounding like a bunch of retired car mechanics the whole time.

They talk about a Man of Steel. An Amazon Princess.

But they never talk about the mean one. The cruel one. The one who couldn't fly or bend steel in his bare hands. The one who scared the crap out of everybody and laughed at all of the rest of us for being the envious cowards we were.

No, they never talk about him. Say his name and watch Dibny's face sag so bad his jaw hits the bar.

Not a man among them wants to hear about Batman.

Was he quietly assassinated? Or did he just decide we weren't worth the grief?

The question hangs in the air for a moment or two, then Jones springs for a round for everybody and himself.

They get talking again. About the old days. The glory days.

They remember.

They were right there. In the thick of it.

Back then.

It wasn't so long ago.

We had heroes.

BOOK ONE

THE DARK KNIGHT RETURNS

I'VE GOT THE HOME STRETCH ALL TO MYSELF WHEN THE READINGS STOP MAKING SENSE. I SWITCH TO MANUAL--

BRUCE, THIS IS *CAROL.* YOU'RE GOING TOO *FAST!*

--BUT THE COMPUTER CROSSES ITS OWN CIRCUITS AND REFUSES TO LET GO. I COAX IT.

IT ISN'T *PROGRAMMED* TO-- BRUCE!

BRUCE, YOU SON OF A *KRRKK*

IT SHOVES HOT NEEDLES IN MY FACE AND TRIES TO MAKE ME BLIND. I'M IN CHARGE NOW AND I LIKE IT.

THEN THE FRONT END LURCHES, ALL WRONG. I KNOW WHAT'S COMING.

I'VE GOT JUST UNDER TWO SECONDS TO SHUT THIS MESS DOWN AND FORFEIT THE RACE.

THE ENGINE, ANGRY, ARGUES THE POINT WITH ME. THE FINISH LINE *IS* **CLOSE,** IT ROARS, TOO CLOSE.

THE LEFT FRONT TIRE DECIDES TO TURN ALL ON ITS OWN. I LAUGH AT IT AND JERK THE STEERING WHEEL TO THE RIGHT.

...BUT NOT GOOD *ENOUGH.*

THE NOSE DIGS UP A CHUNK OF MACADAM. I LOOK AT IT--

--THEN STRAIGHT INTO THE EYE OF THE SUN.

THIS WOULD BE A **GOOD** DEATH...

...*SPECTACULAR* FINISH TO THE NEUMAN ELIMINATION, AS THE FERRIS 6000 *PINWHEELED* ACROSS THE FINISH LINE, A FLAMING COFFIN FOR *BRUCE WAYNE*...

...OR SO EVERYONE *THOUGHT.* TURNS OUT THE MILLIONAIRE *BAILED OUT* AT THE LAST SECOND. SUFFERED ONLY *SUPERFICIAL* BURNS, LOLA?

THANKS, BILL. I'M SURPRISED ANYONE CAN EVEN *THINK* OF SPORTS IN *THIS* WEATHER. RIGHT, DAVE?

RIGHT, LOLA. AT GOTHAM'S MAGNIFICENT TWIN TOWERS IT'S **NINETY-SEVEN**-- WITH NO RELIEF IN SIGHT.

THANKS, DAVE. THIS HEAT WAVE HAS SPARKED MANY ACTS OF CIVIL VIOLENCE HERE IN **GOTHAM CITY**...

...THE MOST **HIDEOUS** OF WHICH HAS TO BE THE BRUTAL SLAYING OF THREE NUNS LAST WEEK BY THE GANG KNOWN AS THE **MUTANTS**.

AND TODAY POLICE FOUND A **DEATH THREAT** NAILED TO THE DOOR OF THE OFFICE OF POLICE COMMISSIONER **JAMES GORDON**.

GORDON, FACING RETIREMENT ON HIS SEVENTIETH BIRTHDAY NEXT MONTH, SPOKE TO A NEWS TWO REPORTER...

I'VE GOT FOUR WEEKS TO NAIL THOSE BASTARDS. IF THIS MEANS THEY'RE WILLING TO TAKE ME ON, I'M DELIGHTED.

IRONICALLY, TODAY ALSO MARKS THE TENTH ANNIVERSARY OF THE LAST RECORDED SIGHTING OF THE **BATMAN**. DEAD OR RETIRED, HIS FATE REMAINS UNKNOWN.

OUR YOUNGER VIEWERS WILL NOT REMEMBER THE **BATMAN**. A RECENT SURVEY SHOWS THAT MOST HIGH SCHOOLERS CONSIDER HIM A **MYTH**.

BUT REAL HE WAS. EVEN TODAY, DEBATE CONTINUES ON THE RIGHT AND WRONG OF HIS ONE-MAN WAR ON CRIME.

THIS REPORTER WOULD LIKE TO THINK THAT HE'S ALIVE AND WELL, ENJOYING A CELEBRATORY DRINK IN THE COMPANY OF FRIENDS...

TO BATMAN, IT'S *GOOD* THAT HE RETIRED-- ISN'T IT?

TINK

I'M GRATEFUL HE *SURVIVED* RETIRING.

HE DIDN'T. BUT *BRUCE WAYNE* IS...ALIVE AND WELL.

GLAD TO HEAR THAT. YOU'VE CERTAINLY LEARNED TO *DRINK*.

REMEMBER THE *OLD DAYS*, BRUCE? THAT PLAYBOY ROUTINE...

YOU WITH YOUR *GINGER ALE*, PRETENDING IT WAS *CHAMPAGNE*, FOOLING EVERYBODY--

--ALMOST.

NOW--WELL, I'D ALMOST *WORRY*.

SPOKEN TO *DICK* LATELY?

NOT FOR *SEVEN* YEARS, JIM. YOU KNOW THAT.

STILL, HUH? I'M DAMN SORRY ABOUT THAT.

ESPECIALLY WITH WHAT HAPPENED TO *JASON*...

LET'S CALL IT A NIGHT, JIM.

WE ARE DAMNED

WE ARE DAMNED

AS WE PART, JIM SQUEEZES MY SHOULDER AND GRINS. "*YOU JUST NEED A WOMAN*," HE SAYS.

...WHILE IN MY GUT THE CREATURE *WRITHES* AND *SNARLS* AND *TELLS* ME WHAT I NEED...

I LEAVE MY CAR IN THE LOT. I CAN'T STAND TO BE INSIDE *ANYTHING* RIGHT NOW. I WALK THE STREETS OF THIS CITY I'M LEARNING TO HATE, THE CITY THAT'S GIVEN *UP*, LIKE THE WHOLE *WORLD* SEEMS TO HAVE.

I'M A *ZOMBIE*. A FLYING *DUTCHMAN*. A *DEAD* MAN, *TEN* YEARS DEAD...

I'LL FEEL BETTER IN THE MORNING. AT LEAST, I'LL FEEL IT **LESS**...

IT'S THE **NIGHT**--WHEN THE CITY'S SMELLS CALL **OUT** TO HIM, THOUGH I LIE BETWEEN SILK SHEETS IN A MILLION-DOLLAR MANSION MILES AWAY...

...WHEN A POLICE SIREN WAKES ME, AND, FOR A MOMENT, I FORGET THAT IT'S ALL OVER...

BUT BATMAN WAS A YOUNG MAN. IF IT WAS REVENGE HE WAS AFTER, HE'S TAKEN IT. IT'S BEEN **FORTY** YEARS SINCE HE WAS BORN...

...BORN HERE.

ONCE AGAIN, HE'S BROUGHT ME **BACK**--TO SHOW ME HOW **LITTLE** IT HAS CHANGED. IT'S OLDER, DIRTIER, BUT--

--IT COULD HAVE HAPPENED YESTERDAY.

IT COULD BE HAPPENING RIGHT NOW.

THEY COULD BE LYING AT YOUR FEET, TWITCHING, BLEEDING...

...AND THE MAN WHO STOLE ALL **SENSE** FROM YOUR LIFE, HE COULD BE STANDING...

...RIGHT OVER THERE...

HE SEES US--

GET AROUND BEHIND HIM--

COME ON, HONEY, SLICE AND DICE--

--I DON'T KNOW, MAN, HE'S AWFUL BIG--

IT IS HIM, IT IS, AND WE KNOW SO MANY WAYS TO HURT HIM...

SO MANY LOVELY WAYS TO **PUNISH** HIM...

NO, IT'S NOT HIM.

SLICE AND DICE, WE GOT A QUOTA--

SO MANY...

I DON'T KNOW, MAN, LOOK AT HIM. HE'S INTO IT--

NOT HIM. HE *FLINCHED* WHEN HE PULLED THE TRIGGER. HE WAS *SICK* AND *GUILTY* OVER WHAT HE DID.

CAN'T DO MURDERS WHEN THEY'RE INTO IT--

ALL HE WANTED WAS *MONEY.* I WAS NAIVE ENOUGH TO THINK HIM THE *LOWEST* SORT OF MAN.

LET'S HIT THE ARCADE, MAN--

THESE--THESE ARE HIS *CHILDREN.* A *PURER* BREED...

--ALWAYS A GOOD TIME AT THE ARCADE--

...AND THIS WORLD IS THEIRS.

...BUTCHERY OF EVERY MEMBER OF THE FAMILY. THE MUTANT ORGANIZATION IS BELIEVED TO HAVE COMMITTED THIS ATROCITY FOR *MONEY* THE FAMILY HAD...

...SOMETHING UNDER TWELVE DOLLARS. THIS IS CONSIDERED A DRUG-RELATED CRIME AT PRESENT, BUT SURELY THIS *HEAT WAVE* IS A FACTOR. RIGHT, DOC?

ABSOLUTELY, BILL. *ROUGH* MONTH IN THE *BIG TOWN.* RIGHT NOW THE MERCURY IS CLIMBING TO AN UNSEASONAL *ONE HUNDRED AND THREE...*

...AND IT LOOKS LIKE IT'S GOING TO GET *WORSE* BEFORE IT GETS BETTER...

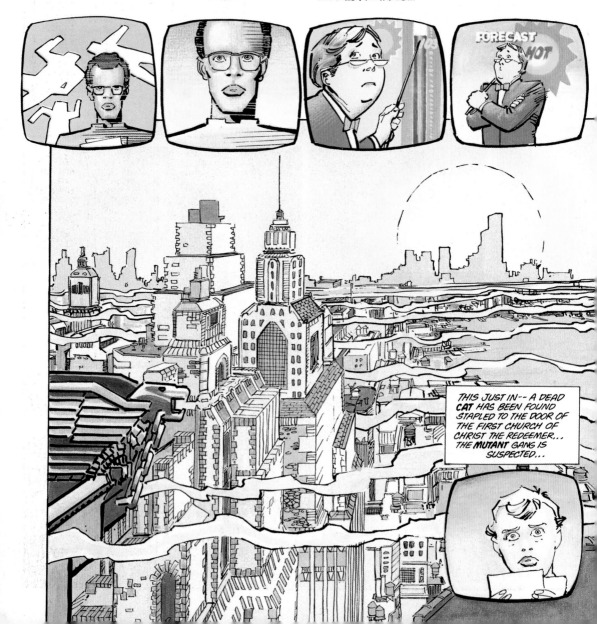

THIS JUST IN-- A DEAD *CAT* HAS BEEN FOUND STAPLED TO THE DOOR OF THE FIRST CHURCH OF CHRIST THE REDEEMER... THE *MUTANT* GANG IS SUSPECTED...

ARKHAM HOME FOR THE EMOTIONALLY TROUBLED

INTENSIVE TREATMENT WARD

NO SMOKING

NINETY-NINE DEGREES AND THE *AIR CONDITIONER* BLOWS...

NO VISITORS

WATER'S OUT IN MY BUILDING, TOO. COULDN'T EVEN TAKE A *SHOWER* THIS MORNING.

YOU KNOW WHAT I HATE MOST ABOUT THE HEAT?

IT'S THE WAY YOUR UNDERWEAR *STICKS* TO--

SHUT UP.

601

YEAH, WELL, YOU DON'T SEE *HIM* SWEATING.

JUST LOOK AT.

YOU LOOK AT HIM.

HE MAKES ME SICK.

YEAH, WELL. GUESS BEING *CRAZY* HAS ITS MOMENTS.

BEEN A LONG TIME SINCE ANY OF *THESE* GUYS HAD MOMENTS.

602

WHEN I *CAME* HERE, THEY SAID--

--I COULD *NEVER* BE CURED.

602

WE KNOW WHAT THEY SAID, HARVEY, BUT THAT'S *HISTORY.* SURGICAL PROCEDURES HAVE *IMPROVED*--

--AS HAVE *PSYCHIATRIC.* YOU'RE FIT TO *RETURN* TO SOCIETY-- NO MATTER WHAT OUR *SEPTUAGENARIAN POLICE COMMISSIONER* SAYS.

MAYBE GORDON...

...IS *RIGHT* ABOUT ME.

NONSENSE, GORDON'S JUST GONE *SENILE.*

DR. *WILLING* ISN'T *QUALIFIED* TO *JUDGE* THAT--

--BUT I *CONCUR.*

THANK YOU, DR. *WOLPER,* AND NOW, *HARVEY DENT*--

--MEET *HARVEY DENT.*

OH, MY *GOD...*

WHAT CAN I SAY?

...THANK YOU, TOM. A NEW LIFE BEGINS TODAY FOR HARVEY DENT.

DENT, A FORMER DISTRICT ATTORNEY, BECAME OBSESSED WITH THE NUMBER *TWO* WHEN HALF HIS FACE WAS SCARRED BY ACID.

DENT BELIEVED HIS DISFIGURATION REVEALED A HIDDEN, EVIL SIDE TO HIS NATURE. HE ADOPTED AS HIS PERSONAL SYMBOL A *DOLLAR COIN*...

...ONE SIDE OF WHICH WAS *DEFACED*, TO REPRESENT THE WARRING SIDES OF HIS SPLIT-PERSONALITY. A FLIP OF THE COIN COULD MEAN LIFE OR DEATH FOR HIS VICTIMS.

DENT'S CRIMES WERE BRILLIANTLY PATHOLOGICAL, THE MOST HORRENDOUS OF WHICH WAS HIS LAST--

--THE KIDNAPPING AND RANSOMING OF *SIAMESE TWINS*, ONE OF WHOM HE ATTEMPTED TO MURDER EVEN AFTER THE RANSOM WAS PAID.

HE WAS APPREHENDED IN THE ACT BY GOTHAM'S FAMOUS VIGILANTE, THE *BATMAN*, AND COMMITTED TO *ARKHAM ASYLUM* TWELVE YEARS AGO.

FOR THE PAST THREE YEARS DENT HAS BEEN TREATED BY *DR. BARTHOLOMEW WOLPER* FOR HIS PSYCHOSIS...

...WHILE NOBEL PRIZE-WINNING PLASTIC SURGEON *DR. HERBERT WILLING* DEDICATED HIMSELF TO RESTORING THE *FACE OF HARVEY DENT.*

SPEAKING TODAY, BOTH DOCTORS WERE *JUBILANT*.

HARVEY'S READY TO LOOK AT THE WORLD AND SAY, "HEY--I'M OKAY."

AND HE LOOKS *GREAT*.

DENT READ A BRIEF STATEMENT TO THE MEDIA...

I DO NOT ASK GOTHAM CITY TO FORGIVE MY CRIMES, I MUST EARN THAT, BY DEDICATING MYSELF TO PUBLIC SERVICE.

FOR ME, THIS IS THE END OF A LONG NIGHT-MARE...AND THE FIRST STEP ON THE LONG ROAD TO ABSOLUTION.

NEXT, DENT DREW FOND APPLAUSE BY PRODUCING A NEWLY-MINTED **DOLLAR COIN.**

IT WAS, OF COURSE, UNMARRED.

BUT POLICE COMMISSIONER JAMES GORDON'S REACTION TO DENT'S RELEASE WAS NOT ENTHUSIASTIC...

NO, I AM **NOT** SATISFIED. DR. WOLPER'S REPORT SEEMS OVERLY **OPTIMISTIC**-- NOT TO MENTION **SLOPPY.**

WHILE MILLIONAIRE **BRUCE WAYNE,** WHO SPONSORED DENT'S TREATMENT, HAD THIS TO SAY...

GORDON'S REMARKS SEEM OVERLY **PESSIMISTIC**-- NOT TO MENTION **RUDE.**

THE COMMISSIONER IS AN EXCELLENT **COP**-- BUT, I THINK, A **POOR** JUDGE OF CHARACTER, WE MUST **BELIEVE** IN HARVEY DENT.

WE MUST BELIEVE THAT OUR PRIVATE DEMONS CAN BE DEFEATED...

...FASTER THAN A RABBIT...

...FASTER THAN A RABBIT, MOM! JUST WATCH!

LOOK AT THAT BOY RUN! WE'VE GOT AN **ATHLETE** ON OUR HANDS!

BRUCE-- WHAT ARE YOU GOING TO **DO** WITH IT WHEN YOU **CATCH**--

DON'T GO IN THAT **HOLE**--

WON'T GET AWAY FROM ME...

BRUCE!

GLIDING WITH **ANCIENT** GRACE...

UNWILLING TO **RETREAT** AS HIS BROTHERS DID...

EYES **GLEAMING**, UNTOUCHED BY LOVE OR JOY OR SORROW...

BREATH **HOT** WITH THE TASTE OF FALLEN FOES...THE STENCH OF **DEAD** THINGS, **DAMNED** THINGS...

SURELY THE **FIERCEST** SURVIVOR-- THE **PUREST** WARRIOR...

GLARING, HATING...

...CLAIMING ME AS HIS **OWN.**

DREAMING...

I WAS ONLY SIX YEARS OLD WHEN THAT HAPPENED. WHEN I FIRST SAW THE CAVE...

...HUGE, EMPTY, SILENT AS A **CHURCH,** WAITING, AS THE **BAT** WAS WAITING.

AND NOW THE **COBWEBS** GROW AND THE DUST **THICKENS** IN HERE AS IT DOES IN **ME**--

--AND HE **LAUGHS** AT ME, **CURSES** ME. CALLS ME A **FOOL.** HE FILLS MY **SLEEP,** HE **TRICKS** ME. BRINGS ME HERE WHEN THE NIGHT IS **LONG** AND MY WILL IS **WEAK.** HE **STRUGGLES** RELENTLESSLY, HATEFULLY, TO BE **FREE**--

I WILL NOT **LET** HIM. I GAVE MY **WORD.**

FOR **JASON.**

NEVER.

NEVER AGAIN.

MASTER BRUCE?

YOU SET OFF THE ALARM, SIR.

THIS *SOMNAMBU-LISM* IS BECOMING A BIT OF A *PROBLEM*, CERTAINLY FOR THOSE OF US WITH A PENCHANT FOR SLEEPING IN OUR *BEDS*.

IT'S THE *SPIRITS*, I SUSPECT. TENDS TO MAKE ONE OVERLY *SENTIMENTAL*.

COME, SIR. HARDLY THE HOUR FOR *ANTIQUES*, IS IT?

... HARDLY, *ALFRED.* SORRY TO WAKE YOU.

IT *IS* HALF PAST THREE ...

MASTER BRUCE. WHATEVER HAPPENED TO YOUR *MUSTACHE?*

FOR ME, THIS IS THE END OF A LONG NIGHT-MARE ... AND THE FIRST STEP ON THE LONG ROAD TO ABSOLUTION.

..., THOSE WERE THE LAST WORDS SPOKEN IN PUBLIC BY HARVEY DENT BEFORE HIS DISAPPEARANCE THIS MORNING.

WHILE POLICE COMMISSIONER GORDON ISSUED AN ALL POINTS BULLETIN FOR DENT, ONE VOICE WAS RAISED IN PROTEST...

... THAT OF *DR. BARTHOLOMEW WOLPER*, DENT'S PSYCHIATRIST...

SO--WHAT DO YOU THINK?

I THINK IT'S TOO DAMN HOT--

--AND I THINK HE SHOULD SEE IT OR FOLD.

GORDON'S REACTION IS ONE OF TEXT BOOK HYSTERIA...

I MEAN *DENT* --NOT *DIP STICK* HERE.

SO DO I. OUGHTTA SEE IT OR FOLD.

WE BEEN GETTING BY WITHOUT HIM.

UH HUH.

...AND CHARACTERISTIC INSENSITIVITY. HARVEY, ON THE OTHER HAND, IS AN EXTREMELY SENSITIVE MAN...

I MEAN, IT AIN'T BEEN *GREAT*...

THAT'S RIGHT.

...IN EXTREMELY VULNERABLE EMOTIONAL CONDITION, I BELIEVE...

TONIGHT'S PRESENTATION OF HOLLYWOOD'S FINEST...

...TYRONE POWER IN "THE MARK OF ZORRO"...

ZORRO. I SHOULD HAVE CHECKED THE *LISTINGS*. I SHOULD TURN IT *OFF*-- RIGHT THIS *SECOND*--

--JUST A *MOVIE*. THAT'S ALL IT IS. NO HARM IN WATCHING A MOVIE...

YOU LOVED IT SO *MUCH*...YOU JUMPED AND DANCED LIKE A *FOOL*...YOU REMEMBER...

...YOU REMEMBER THAT *NIGHT*--

RRRMMMM BBBLLLLL

...POWER LINES ARE DOWN ALL OVER THE SUBURBS. IT'S A MEAN ONE-- AND IT'S HEADED STRAIGHT FOR GOTHAM.

LIKE THE WRATH OF GOD IT'S HEADED FOR GOTHAM...

...STRAIGHT OUT OF NOWHERE THIS COMES. AND HAVE I MY UMBRELLA?

SURELY NOT, AND HAD I MY UMBRELLA WOULD IT NOW BE RAINING?

SURELY NOT--

HEY, MOMMIE...

...COME IN HERE WHERE IT'S WARM,

I NEED YOU, MOMMIE.

MAKE ME FEEL SAFE.

OH NO PLEASE...

PLEASE GOD NO--

TALK SOFT...

AAA--

KRMBL KKKKRRAKKKK

GET YOU UGLY ASS IN THERE, BITCH. WE TAKIN A RIDE.

MAN, I UFF!

YOU PAININ ME, YOU MESSIN WIF MY LIVELIHOOD.

NOT MY FACE, SILK... PLEASE...

AAAAH--) LOOKIT YOU, JOANNIE. YOU WENT AN GREW ANOTHER NOSTRIL.

HEY, MAN--TAKE IT SOMEPLACE ELSE. I DON'T NEED THE GRIEF.

SHUT YOU HAIRY FACE AN DRIVE.

YEAH. ALL RIGHT. JUST MAKE IT QUICK.

...BREAKTHROUGH IN HAIR REPLACEMENT TECHNIQUES, AND THAT'S THE-- EXCUSE ME...

I'VE JUST BEEN HANDED THIS BULLETIN-- A LARGE, *BAT-LIKE* CREATURE HAS BEEN SIGHTED ON GOTHAM'S SOUTH SIDE.

IT IS SAID TO HAVE ATTACKED AND SERIOUSLY INJURED THREE *CAT-BURGLARS* WHO HAVE PLAGUED THAT NEIGHBORHOOD

YOU DON'T SUPPOSE...

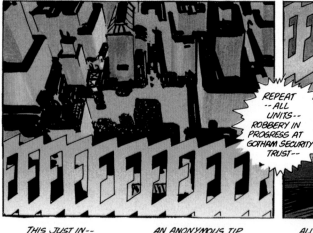

REPEAT --ALL UNITS-- ROBBERY IN PROGRESS AT GOTHAM SECURITY TRUST--

THERE THEY *ARE*, KID. LET'S *MOTORVATE.*

THIS JUST IN-- TWO YOUNG CHILDREN WHO DISAPPEARED THIS MORNING HAVE BEEN FOUND UNHARMED IN A RIVERSIDE WAREHOUSE.

AN ANONYMOUS TIP LED POLICE TO THE WAREHOUSE, WHERE THEY FOUND THE CHILDREN WITH SIX MEMBERS OF THE *MUTANT* GANG.

ALL SIX ARE SUFFERING FROM MULTIPLE CUTS, CONTUSIONS, AND BROKEN BONES. THEY WERE RUSHED TO GOTHAM GENERAL HOSPITAL.

THE CHILDREN DESCRIBED AN ATTACK ON THE GANG MEMBERS BY A HUGE MAN DRESSED LIKE *DRACULA...*

THAT *JALOPY*—IT PULLED AWAY FROM THE BANK AT THE SAME—

HELL WITH *THAT.* THE *CUSTOM* JOB'S GOT TO BE *OUR BABY*...

POLICE PHONE LINES ARE *JAMMED* WITH CITIZENS DESCRIBING WHAT SEEMS TO BE A *SIEGE* ON GOTHAM'S UNDERWORLD...

...BY THE *BATMAN*.

ALTHOUGH SEVERAL RESCUED VICTIMS-TO-BE HAVE DESCRIBED THE VIGILANTE TO *NEWS TWELVE* REPORTERS...

...COMMISSIONER JAMES GORDON HAS DECLINED TO COMMENT ON WHETHER OR NOT THIS MIGHT MEAN THE *RETURN* OF THE *BATMAN*...

GORDON'LL HAVE OUR *HEADS* IF WE LOSE THEM...

DAMN—THAT SUCKER CAN *MOVE!*

HEY, WHAT'S *THAT?*

WHAT'S WHAT? I CAN'T—

UP AHEAD—IT'S— SOMETHING *WEIRD*...

KID—THIS AIN'T THE *TIME*—

BUT IT'S—

ALL RIGHT! ALL RIGHT! WHAT *IS*—

HOLY...

...*BATTERED, WOUNDED* CRIMINALS ARE BEING FOUND BY POLICE—WHILE WITNESSES' DESCRIPTIONS ARE *CONFUSED* AND *CONFLICTING*...

YOU'RE *SLOWING DOWN!*

HEH. YEAH. WE'RE IN FOR A *SHOW*, KID.

...MOST DESCRIPTIONS SEEM TO MATCH THE *METHOD* AND *APPEARANCE* OF THE *BATMAN*—OR AT LEAST THE *IMPRESSION* HE WAS KNOWN TO *MAKE*...

...COULDN'T BE BATMAN. TURK SAID HE *KILLED* BATMAN.

TURK SAYS *LOTS.*

FOUR OF THEM. ONE IN THE CAR, LEG BROKEN, IN SHOCK.

HARD TO *SEE*--

QUIET!

OTHER THREE ARE ARMED-- AND SMART ENOUGH TO HANG CLOSE TOGETHER.

BUT THEY'RE *SCARED.*

FLOOR'S *WEAK.* DOESN'T FEEL *SAFE*--

SO LIVE DANGEROUS-LY.

AND SHUT *UP.*

IF IT *IS* HIM...

..., HE'S GOT TO BE PRETTY *OLD*...

SHHH!

OLD ENOUGH TO NEED MY *LEGS* TO CLIMB A ROPE...

KRFEE

OVER THERE--

FIRE *LOW*--

BLAMBLAM BLAMBLAM

THEY'RE *FAST.*

BLAMBLAM BLAMBLAM

SHOULDN'T HAVE GONE SO EASY ON THEM IN THE CAR.

WE *GET* HIM?

HARD TO *TELL.* HAVE TO ASSUME WE *DIDN'T.*

WAIT. WHAT'S THAT *SOUND*...

GGGRRRR

...KILL HIM I'LL *KILL* HIM...

THE LAST ONES USUALLY THE ONE TO LOSE IT. SO I LET HIM.

AND I LET HIM COME TO ME.

THEN I HEAR THE ROOKIE'S FOOTSTEPS, COMING UP FAST BEHIND ME.

I'LL HAVE TO KEEP HIM FROM GETTING KILLED.

EVERYBODY *FREEZ*

OWW!

THE ROOKIE'S SAFE FOR THE FIVE SECONDS IT WILL TAKE HIM TO FIND HIS PISTOL.

I PLAY THE SHADOWS, FORCING THE HOOD TO COME CLOSE. HE MAKES LESS NOISE THAN A TRUCK.

THERE ARE SEVEN WORKING DEFENSES FROM THIS POSITION.

THREE OF THEM DISARM WITH MINIMAL CONTACT.

THREE OF THEM KILL.

THE OTHER--

--HURTS.

YOU'RE UNDER ARREST, MISTER.

YOU'VE *CRIPPLED* THAT MAN!

HE'S YOUNG. HE'LL PROBABLY WALK AGAIN.

BUT HE'LL STAY *SCARED*-- WON'T YOU, PUNK?

JESUS SWEET *JESUS*...

...ONE ALMOST EXPECTS TO SEE THE BAT-SIGNAL STRIKING THE SIDE OF ONE OF GOTHAM'S TWIN TOWERS. YES, HE GAVE US QUITE A NIGHT...

SURE KEPT THE *HOSPITALS* BUSY.

YES, MORRIE. BUT I THINK IT'S A MISTAKE...

...TO THINK OF THIS IN PURELY *POLITICAL* TERMS...

BB...

RATHER, I REGARD IT AS A SYMBOLIC RESURGENCE OF THE COMMON MAN'S WILL TO RESIST...

BBBAT...

A REBIRTH OF THE AMERICAN *FIGHTING* SPIRIT.

BATMAN.

EASE *UP*, LANA. THE ONLY THING HE SIGNIFIES...

...IS AN ABERRANT PSYCHOTIC *FORCE*--

DARLING.

-- MORALLY *BANKRUPT*, POLITICALLY *HAZARDOUS*, REACTIONARY *PARANOID*--

--A *DANGER* TO EVERY CITIZEN OF *GOTHAM!*

PERHAPS, MORRIE. PERHAPS THE BATMAN *IS* DANGER-OUS...

...BUT HE'S HARDLY AS DANGEROUS AS HIS ENEMIES, IS HE? TAKE HARVEY DENT, JUST TO PICK A NAME...

THAT'S CUTE, LANA, BUT HARDLY APROPOS. AND HARDLY FAIR TO AS TROUBLED A SOUL AS HARVEY DENT'S.

HE CERTAINLY IS TROUBLE FOR HIS VICTIMS.

WAS, LANA. WAS. IF HARVEY DENT IS RETURNING TO CRIME -- AND PLEASE NOTE THAT I SAID IF -- IT GOES WITHOUT SAYING THAT HE'S NOT IN CONTROL OF HIMSELF.

AND BATMAN IS?

CERTAINLY. HE KNOWS EXACTLY WHAT HE'S DOING. HIS KIND OF SOCIAL FASCIST ALWAYS DOES.

THEN WHY DO YOU CALL HIM PSYCHOTIC? BECAUSE YOU LIKE TO USE THAT WORD FOR ANY MOTIVE THAT'S TOO BIG FOR YOUR LITTLE MIND? BECAUSE HE FIGHTS CRIME INSTEAD OF PERPETRATING IT?

YOU DON'T CALL EXCESSIVE FORCE A CRIME? HOW ABOUT ASSAULT, FAT LADY? OR BREAKING AND ENTERING? HUH? TRY RECKLESS EN

DNG

SORRY, MORRIE, BUT WE'RE OUT OF TIME -- THOUGH I'M SURE THIS DEBATE IS FAR FROM OVER. FOR THOSE OF YOU WHO CAME IN LATE, TODAY'S POINT VERSUS POINT...

...WAS CONCERNED WITH LAST NIGHT'S ATTACK ON DOZENS OF INDIVIDUALS WHO MAY HAVE BEEN CRIMINALS BY A PARTY OR PARTIES WHO MAY HAVE BEEN THE BATMAN.

ALSO OF CONCERN IS THIS MORNING'S ANNOUNCEMENT BY POLICE MEDIA RELATIONS DIRECTOR LOUIS GALLAGHER THAT A DEFACED DOLLAR COIN, WAS FOUND ON ONE OF THE SUSPECTS...

...IN LAST NIGHT'S PAYROLL ROBBERY. THOSE WHO REMEMBER THE CRIMES OF HARVEY DENT WILL RECOGNIZE THIS AS HIS TRADEMARK.

POLICE COMMISSIONER GORDON HAS REFUSED TO CONFIRM THAT HE HAS ISSUED AN ARREST ORDER...

SCREW THE PRESS!

JAMES W. GORDON
COMMISSIONER OF POLICE

STILL HOT ON THE HEELS OF BATMAN'S APPARENT RETURN...

NO MORE LEAKS, GALLAGHER--OR I'LL HAVE YOUR HEAD ON A STICK!

SON OF A...

...THIS DOES GIVE ONE A SENSE OF DEJA VU...

TURN THAT GOD DAMNED THING OFF, MERKEL.

A SAD, STRANGE CRIMINAL WAS HARVEY

COMMISSIONER, IF YOU PLEASE...

WE WILL KILL THE OLD MAN GORDON. HIS WOMEN WILL WEEP FOR HIM. WE WILL CHOP HIM. WE WILL GRIND HIM. WE WILL BATHE IN HIS BLOOD.

I MYSELF WILL KILL THE FOOL BATMAN. I WILL RIP THE MEAT FROM HIS BONES AND SUCK THEM DRY. I WILL EAT HIS HEART AND DRAG HIS BODY THROUGH THE STREET.

DON'T CALL US A GANG. DON'T CALL US CRIMINALS. WE ARE THE LAW. WE ARE THE FUTURE. GOTHAM CITY BELONGS TO THE MUTANTS. SOON THE WORLD WILL BE OURS.

WITH THAT VIDEOTAPED MESSAGE, THE MUTANT LEADER -- WHOSE NAME AND FACE REMAIN A SECRET -- HAS DECLARED WAR ON THE CITY OF GOTHAM... AND ON ITS MOST FAMOUS CHAMPION...

THE ROOM IS SPLIT BETWEEN LIGHT AND DARK, CLEAN AND DIRTY. BUT THE SPLIT ISN'T EVEN -- IT FAVORS THE DIRTY.

IT'S AS IF THE DARK SIDE IS CLAIMING THE ROOM... AS IT CLAIMED THE COIN...

FACE -- IT WAS BATMAN. HE --

WH...

YOUR BOSS LEFT. HE KNEW I'D TRACK HIM.

SLAM

IF HE IS HARVEY DENT, HE'S A MENACE TO EVERY LIFE IN GOTHAM.

I KNOW YOU'RE VERY CONCERNED ABOUT THAT.

GET AWAY FROM ME...

YOU'RE GOING TO TELL ME EVERYTHING YOU KNOW, SOONER OR LATER.

IF IT'S LATER --

-- I WON'T MIND.

NO! -- STAY BACK --

-- I GOT RIGHTS --

YOU'VE GOT RIGHTS.

LOTS OF RIGHTS.

SOMETIMES I *COUNT* THEM JUST TO MAKE MYSELF FEEL *CRAZY.*

BUT RIGHT NOW YOU'VE GOT A PIECE OF GLASS SHOVED INTO A MAJOR ARTERY IN YOUR ARM.

RIGHT NOW YOU'RE BLEED-ING TO DEATH.

RIGHT NOW I'M THE ONLY ONE IN THE WORLD WHO CAN GET YOU TO A HOSPITAL IN TIME.

BATMAN? YEAH, I THINK HE'S A-OKAY. HE'S KICKING JUST THE RIGHT BUTTS -- BUTTS THE COPS AIN'T KICKING, THAT'S FOR SURE. HOPE HE GOES AFTER THE HOMOS NEXT.

MAKES ME SICK. WE MUST TREAT THE SOCIALLY MIS-ORIENTED WITH *REHABILITATIVE* METHODS. WE MUST PATIENT-LY REALIGN THEIR-- EXCUSE ME--? NO, I'D NEVER LIVE IN THE CITY...

...CAN'T *BELIEVE* YOU HAD IT PUT *BACK,* COMMISSIONER. IF *GALLAGHER* KNEW...

GALLAGHER DOESN'T RUN THIS DEPART-MENT *YET,* MERKEL!

KOFF

BUT ISN'T THERE SOME *OTHER* WAY TO CALL HIM?

AT LEAST A *DOZEN.*

THEN *WHY?*

TO LET THEM *KNOW,* MERKEL, TO LET *EVERYONE* KNOW.

HIT IT.

OBVIOUSLY A FASCIST. NEVER *HEARD* OF CIVIL RIGHTS.

AND DOESN'T THE TV JUST *LOVE* HIM.

THEY *ALL* LOVE HIM. THE AMERICAN CONSCIENCE DIED WITH THE KENNEDYS.

TOO TRUE...

ALL THE MARCHING WE DID -- IT'S LIKE IT NEVER *HAPPENED,* NOW.

I KNOW... I KNOW...

SOMETIMES I *DESPAIR...*

GIVE ME *ANOTHER HIT* OF THAT, HUH?

--SO IT'S JUST A MATTER OF FIGURING OUT WHAT HE'S AFTER.

THE PAYROLL ROBBERY WAS COMMITTED TO SPONSOR IT.

SPONSOR IT? THAT DOESN'T MAKE SENSE.

TWO HELICOPTERS WERE STOLEN TODAY. ONE, A STATE-OF-THE-ART MILITARY FIGHTER-- THE OTHER, AN OLD ARMY SURPLUS JOB. THAT'S GOT TO BE DENT'S WORK.

WITH THAT PAYROLL HE COULD HAVE BOUGHT THEM.

THEN IT'S GOING TO BE A CRIME BY AIR-- USING SOMETHING ELSE MORE COSTLY.

HE'S NOT CAREFUL, WHOEVER HE IS.

YOU STILL DON'T THINK IT'S DENT?

I HOPE NOT. HARVEY WRESTLED LONG AND HARD WITH HIS OTHER SIDE. TO HAVE IT DEVOUR HIM NOW...

BUT IF IT IS...

"TWICE AS BIG AS YOU CAN IMAGINE" --THAT'S ALL HE HAD TO SAY?

THAT'S ALL HE KNEW, JIM.

BUT TOMORROW IS THE SECOND-- AND A TUESDAY--

IF IT'S HARVEY, WE'LL CATCH HIM... THE TRICK WILL BE TO KEEP HIM ALIVE. HE'S POSSESSED, JIM. OUT OF CONTROL.

I THINK HE WANTS TO DIE.

WE ARE TALKING ABOUT HARVEY DENT...

IT SHOULDN'T BE DIFFICULT TO FIND HIS TARGET. ACCESSIBLE BY HELICOPTER AND TWICE AS BIG AS...

...TWICE AS BIG...

YES, MERV. I AM CONVINCED OF HARVEY'S INNOCENCE. ABSOLUTELY. HOWEVER, I WON'T GO SO FAR AS TO SAY I'M SURE HE HASN'T RETURNED TO CRIME.

I KNOW THAT SOUNDS CONFUSING. THESE THINGS OFTEN DO TO THE LAYMAN. BUT I'LL TRY TO EXPLAIN WITHOUT GETTING OVERLY TECHNICAL.. YOU SEE, IT ALL GETS DOWN TO THIS BATMAN FELLOW.

BATMAN'S PSYCHOTIC SUBLIMATIVE / PSYCHO-EROTIC BEHAVIOR PATTERN IS LIKE A NET. WEAK-EGOED NEUROTICS, LIKE HARVEY, ARE DRAWN INTO CORRESPONDING INTERSTICING PATTERNS,

YOU MIGHT SAY BATMAN COMMITS THE CRIMES... USING HIS SO-CALLED VILLAINS AS NARCISSISTIC PROXIES...

ALL THE OTHER GUYS'D GIVEN UP ON YOU, BOSS.

BUT I KNEW YOU WAS GONNA BE OKAY. YOU LOOK GOOD...

BET YOU GOT SOME KINDA KEEN ESCAPE PLANNED. WELL, YOU CAN COUNT ON ME, BUT...

...BUT I GOT A PROBLEM.

YOU KNOW I LIKE TO MAKE STUFF. IT'S ALL I'M GOOD AT...

...WELL HARVEY DENT WANTS TO PAY ME A LOT OF MONEY TO MAKE HIM SOME BOMBS.

HE NEEDS THEM TONIGHT-- THAT'S IF I'M GOING TO MAKE THEM...

I HAVEN'T SAID YES YET...

WHAT KIND OF BOMBS?

ONE MORE TIME I CHECK MY UTILITY BELT.

NERVE GAS AMPULES. FREEZING COMPOUND. CABLE. GRAPPLING HOOKS. STETHOSCOPE. PAIN KILLERS.

NONE OF IT'S GONE ANYWHERE IN THE LAST TEN MINUTES.

I SHIFT MY LEGS TO KEEP THEM FROM CRAMPING AND WATCH NIGHT SETTLE LIKE A CEASE FIRE ON THE CITY OF GOTHAM.

THEN I HEAR IT.

UP WHUP WHUP WHUP WHUP WHUP WHUP WHUP

DENT--OR WHOEVER --IS SURE TO BE IN THE NEWER COPTER. I'M HOPING HE'LL LAND ON THE TOWER I PICKED...

BUT I'M NOT COUNTING ON IT.

POKITAPOKITAP OKITAPOKITAPO

THEY SPLIT. THE ARMY SURPLUS JOB SETTLES DOWN, SPUTTERING LIKE A CRANKY OLD MAN BEHIND ME.

I PICKED THE WRONG ROOF.

GOOD THING I BROUGHT THE GUN.

THE NEW ONE COMES IN LOW, A GLEAMING METAL DRAGONFLY.

I'LL HAVE TO BUY ONE OF THOSE...

WHUP WHUP

...BROADCAST LIVE FROM GOTHAM'S TWIN TOWERS, IT'S NEWS TWO...

NEWS 2

GOOD EVENING. I'M LOLA CHONG. TONIGHT WE'RE PLEASED TO BRING YOU A SPECIAL REPORT...

PAIN THAT'S THREE DAYS OLD CRAWLS ACROSS MY BACK. I KICK THE DUST FROM MY JOINTS AND CLIMB. IT USED TO BE EASIER.

...BATMAN: CRUSADER OR MENACE? GOTHAM'S LIVING LEGEND THROUGH THE EYES OF THE VERY FEW WHO-- WHAT IN--

PLEASE STAND BY. WE ARE EXPERIENCING TECHNICAL DIFFICULTIES.

WHATEVER HE'S GOT IN MIND, HE WANTS IT PUBLIC--

TOO BAD I CAN'T GIVE HIM MY ATTENTION. NOT JUST YET.

THIS STUFF HAS A NAME THAT'S AS LONG AS YOUR ARM.

IT WAS DEVELOPED BY THE MILITARY DURING ONE OF OUR MORE CONTEMPTIBLE WARS.

HEY--

IT CONCENTRATES A POWERFUL STIMULANT TO A SECTION OF THE RIGHT **HEMISPHERE** OF YOUR BRAIN.

A STRONG DOSE AND YOU **DIE** OF **FRIGHT** IN **FIFTEEN** SECONDS.

A LIGHT DOSE, LIKE THIS--

--AND YOU SPEND TWENTY OR THIRTY MINUTES RELIVING YOUR LEAST FAVORITE **NIGHTMARE.**

THE ONLY AFTER EFFECT I'VE NOTICED IS A MARKED AVERSION TO GUNS, KNIVES AND CRIME-FIGHTERS...

AS I SUSPECTED -- A BOMB.

WITH ENOUGH CHARGE TO DEMOLISH THE BUILDING.

APPARENTLY A DETONATOR JOB. THAT WOULD MAKE SENSE.

WAIT--IF THOSE READINGS MEAN WHAT I THINK THEY DO...

AM I ON?

THE IGNITION PROCESS HAS ALREADY STARTED. IT COULD BLOW ANY SECOND.

SOMEBODY WENT TO THE TROUBLE OF DISGUISING IT, BUT WHY? AND WHO?

PEOPLE OF GOTHAM--LET ME APOLOGIZE RIGHT OFF THE BAT FOR THE INTERRUPTION OF YOUR VIEWING PLEASURE. THIS IS HARVEY DENT SPEAKING.

BRILLIANT DESIGN--WORTHY OF THE JOKER.

I'M NOT UP ON THESE DIGITAL JOBS...

I STAND HERE ATOP GOTHAM'S BEAUTIFUL TWIN TOWERS, WITH TWO BOMBS CAPABLE OF MAKING THEM RUBBLE. YOU HAVE TWENTY MINUTES TO SAVE THEM.

SO I FREEZE IT. AND IF I HAD THE TIME OR THE RIGHT--

-- I'D SAY A PRAYER.

THE PRICE IS FIVE MILLION DOLLARS. I WOULD HAVE MADE IT TWO -- BUT I'VE GOT BILLS TO PAY...

TEN SECONDS LATER BOTH THE BUILDING AND I ARE STANDING AND EXACTLY THAT MUCH IS RIGHT IN THE WORLD. I TAKE IN THE ACTION ON THE OTHER SIDE.

HE'S TAPPED INTO THE TV ANTENNA--NO DOUBT RANSOMING THE LIVES OF THOUSANDS-- WHILE THE TIMER HE DOESN'T KNOW ABOUT IS MOMENTS AWAY FROM TAKING IT ALL OUT OF HIS HANDS. HARVEY, IF IT IS YOU--YOU'VE HAD EVERY CHANCE THERE IS.

HE'S GOT YOUR STYLE, HARVEY, AND YOUR GUTS.

BLAM BLAM

UNFORTUNATELY FOR HIM, HE'S GOT NO MORE SENSE OF SELF-PRESERVATION THAN YOU DID...

BLAM

...AND INSPIRES THE SAME LEVEL OF LOYALTY FROM HIS MEN.

IT TAKES NEARLY A MINUTE TO FALL FROM THIS HEIGHT. AND DESPITE WHAT YOU MAY HAVE HEARD, YOU'RE LIKELY TO STAY CONSCIOUS ALL THE WAY DOWN.

THOUGHTS LIKE THAT KEEP ME WARM AT NIGHT.

NOT MUCH OF A CORPSE LEFT.

MOSTLY LIQUID.

PROBLEM IS...

THE IMPACT IS TREMENDOUS. EVEN BONE IS TURNED TO POWDER.

...THERE MIGHT NOT BE ANY FINGER-PRINTS.

EVEN DENTAL RECORDS WOULD PROBABLY BE USELESS.

AND LIKE I SAID, HARVEY...

...I HAVE TO KNOW.

WE TUMBLE LIKE LOVERS.

THE AIR IS COLD.

THE NIGHT IS SILENT.

LEAVING THE WORLD NO POORER--

--FOUR MEN DIE.

THE DARK KNIGHT TRIUMPHANT

PROBLEM WITH CRIME IS THE MORE YOU *KNOW*, THE MORE *NERVOUS* IT MAKES YOU.

ME, I CAN'T LOOK AT THAT *DOORWAY* OVER THERE WITHOUT THINKING OF THE SEVENTY-TWO *CORPSES* I'VE FOUND IN SPOTS LIKE THAT...

...SHOT OR *STABBED* OR JUST *BEATEN* TO *DEATH* BECAUSE THEY WERE TOO *STUPID* TO KEEP THEIR DISTANCE.

TOO STUPID, OR TOO *CIVILIZED*. ONE'S THE SAME AS THE OTHER IN *GOTHAM CITY*.

I PASS A *LIQUOR STORE*, RUN MY EYES OVER THE RIGID FEATURES OF THE HUNK OF METAL THAT USED TO BE A FRIENDLY *MERCHANT*.

I WONDER HOW MANY MEN HE'S HAD TO *KILL*, JUST TO STAY IN BUSINESS.

I SEE A HIGH-PRICED *CAR*, GLEAMING LIKE *NEW* IN THE STREETLIGHT, ONCE A SYMBOL OF *WEALTH* AND *POWER*, NOW JUST ANOTHER *TARGET* IN A CITY OF *VICTIMS*.

A YOUNG BOY DASHES PAST ME, HEALTHY, DIRTY, AND *BEAUTIFUL*. YOU DON'T WANT TO KNOW WHAT HE MAKES ME THINK OF.

I CURSE *SARAH*, NOT MEANING IT, FOR HER HIPPIE VEGETARIAN RECIPES AND THE *BEAN SPROUTS* SHE FORGOT TO PICK UP.

THEN MY *CIGAR* DOES ITS USUAL AND I COUGH UP A LOAD OF THE *BROWN STUFF*.

I'M *AMAZED*--AS MY *HEAD* GOES LIGHT AND THE *SPOTS* DANCE IN FRONT OF ME-- THAT SHE CONVINCED ME NOT TO *SMOKE* IN MY OWN HOME.

THEN I SUCK IT AGAIN.

DYING NEVER SEEMED REAL TO ME WHEN I WAS YOUNG...

FOR SOME REASON I WANT TO SEE *BRUCE* --NOT TO *TALK*...I MEAN SURE, TO *TALK*, AND MAYBE TO *DRINK*, EVEN THOUGH HE SEEMS TO HAVE GIVEN THAT UP.

SUDDENLY THE *HAIR* BRISTLES ON THE BACK OF MY NECK.

I HEAR A GIRLISH *GIGGLE* AND THE COLD, OILED SOUND OF A *GUN* BEING COCKED BEHIND ME.

I SEE THE FACE OF A KILLER WHO ISN'T YET OLD ENOUGH TO *SHAVE*.

SOME ROBIN. I FIGURE.

COMMISSIONER-- YOU JUST SHOT A BOY. HOW DOES THAT FEEL? COMMISSIONER?...

THANK YOU, HERNANDO. THIS IS THE THIRD ATTEMPT ON GORDON'S LIFE IN THE THREE WEEKS SINCE THE LEADER OF THE MUTANT ORGANIZATION MADE HIS VIDEOTAPED DEATH TREAT...

WE WILL KILL THE OLD MAN GORDON. HIS WOMEN WILL WEEP FOR HIM. WE WILL CHOP HIM. WE WILL GRIND HIM. WE WILL BATHE IN HIS BLOOD.

I MYSELF WILL KILL THE FOOL BATMAN. I WILL RIP THE MEAT FROM HIS BONES AND SUCK THEM DRY. I WILL EAT HIS HEART AND DRAG HIS BODY THROUGH THE STREET.

DON'T CALL US A GANG. DON'T CALL US CRIMINALS. WE ARE THE LAW. WE ARE THE FUTURE. GOTHAM CITY BELONGS TO THE MUTANTS. SOON THE WORLD WILL BE OURS.

GORDON, FACING MANDATORY RETIREMENT LATER THIS WEEK, HAS OFFERED TO STAY AT THE JOB UNTIL THE MUTANT CRISIS HAS BEEN RESOLVED. POLICE MEDIA RELATIONS DIRECTOR LOUIS GALLAGHER HAD THIS TO SAY...

NICE OF JIM TO OFFER, BUT I THINK WE ALL KNOW THINGS'LL COOL OUT ONCE HE STEPS DOWN. THE MUTANTS HAVE A THING ABOUT HIM...NO, I THINK IT'S TIME FOR NEW BLOOD...

STRANGELY, THAT "NEW BLOOD" HAS YET TO BE OFFICIALLY ANNOUNCED. WHILE INSPECTOR JOHN DALE SEEMS TO BE THE OBVIOUS CHOICE, THE MAYOR HAS YET TO COMMIT HIMSELF...

I'M STILL POOLING OPINIONS. I'M STILL POOLING OPINIONS.

WITH A SCANT SIX HOURS REMAINING, THE QUESTIONS HANG IN THE AIR-- WHO WILL REPLACE JIM GORDON? AND WHAT WILL BECOME THE OFFICIAL POSITION ON THE BATMAN? TOM?

GOOD QUESTION, LOLA. MRS. JOYCE RIDLEY WAS ADMITTED TO A PRIVATE HOSPITAL UPSTATE FOR PSYCHIATRIC OBSERVATION FOLLOWING HER COLLAPSE THIS MORNING.

HER TEN-MONTH BABY, KEVIN, HEIR TO THE RIDLEY CHEWING GUM FORTUNE, IS STILL MISSING. ANYONE WITH INFORMATION IS URGED TO CALL THE CRISIS HOTLINE...

I BELIEVE YOU.

...A RUTHLESS, MONSTROUS VIGILANTE, STRIKING AT THE FOUNDATIONS OF OUR DEMOCRACY--MALICIOUSLY OPPOSED TO THE PRINCIPLES THAT MAKE OURS THE MOST NOBLE NATION IN THE WORLD-- AND THE KINDEST...

...FRANKLY, I'M SURPRISED THERE AREN'T A HUNDRED LIKE HIM OUT THERE-- A THOUSAND PEOPLE ARE FED UP WITH TERROR-- WITH STUPID LAWS AND SOCIAL COWARDICE. HE'S ONLY TAKING BACK WHAT'S OURS...

THESE--AND MANY, MANY OTHERS-- ARE THE REACTIONS TO A PHENOMENON THAT HAS STRUCK A NERVE CENTER IN OUR SOCIETY-- THE RETURN OF THE BATMAN.

TONIGHT, WE WILL EXAMINE HIS IMPACT ON OUR CONSCIOUSNESS. FROM METROPOLIS-- WE HAVE LANA LANG, MANAGING EDITOR OF THE DAILY PLANET...

...JOINING US FROM GOTHAM CITY-- DR. BARTHOLEMEW WOLPER, POPULAR PSYCHOLOGIST AND SOCIAL SCIENTIST, AUTHOR OF THE BEST-SELLING "HEY--I'M OKAY"...

...WITH US TONIGHT FROM HIS OFFICE IN WASHINGTON-- PRESIDENTIAL MEDIA ADVISOR CHUCK BRICK.

DR. WOLPER--YOU HAVE CLAIMED THAT THE BATMAN IS HIMSELF RESPONSIBLE FOR THE CRIMES HE FIGHTS. STILL, CRIME RATES HAVE SHOWN A STEADY DROP IN THE WEEKS SINCE HIS RETURN. HOW DO YOU EXPLAIN THIS?

I'M GLAD YOU ASKED ME THAT QUESTION, TED. IT IS TRUE THAT THIS BATMAN HAS TERRORIZED THE ECONOMICALLY DIS- ADVANTAGED AND SOCIALLY MISALIGNED--BUT HIS EFFECTS ARE FAR FROM POSITIVE.

PICTURE THE PUBLIC PSYCHE AS A VAST, MOIST MEMBRANE --THROUGH THE MEDIA, BATMAN HAS STRUCK THIS MEMBRANE A VICIOUS BLOW, AND IT HAS RECOILED. HENCE YOUR MISLEADING STATISTICS.

BUT YOU SEE, TED, THE MEMBRANE IS FLEXIBLE-- AND PERMEABLE. HERE THE MORE SIGNIFICANT EFFECTS OF THE BLOW BECOME CALCULABLE, EVEN PREDICTABLE. TO WIT--

EVERY ANTI-SOCIAL ACT CAN BE TRACED TO *IRRESPONSIBLE MEDIA INPUT.* GIVEN THIS, THE PRESENCE OF SUCH AN ABERRANT, VIOLENT FORCE IN THE MEDIA CAN ONLY LEAD TO ANTI-SOCIAL *PROGRAMMING.*

JUST AS *HARVEY DENT*-- WHO'S RECOVERING STEADILY, THANKS FOR ASKING-- ASSUMED THE ROLE OF *IDEOLOGICAL DOPPELGANGER* TO THE BATMAN, SO A WHOLE NEW *GENERATION,* CONFUSED AND ANGRY--

-- WILL BE BENT TO THE MATRIX OF BATMAN'S PATHOLOGICAL SELF-DELUSION. BATMAN IS, IN THIS CONTEXT-- AND PARDON THE TERM-- A SOCIAL *DISEASE...*

THAT'S THE *DUMBEST* LOAD OF...

LANA-- PLEASE-- THE *NETWORK*--

DIDN'T *SUCK.*

MR. BRICK--THE PRESIDENT HAS REMAINED *SILENT* ON THIS ISSUE. DON'T YOU--AND HE--FEEL THAT THE NATIONAL *UPROAR* OVER THE BATMAN WARRANTS, IF NOT ACTION, A STATEMENT OF *POSITION?*

HECK, TED. HE'LL GET AROUND TO A *PRESS CONFERENCE* SOONER OR LATER. BUT THE PRESIDENT'S GOT TO KEEP HIS EYE ON THE *BIG PICTURE,* Y'KNOW? AND THIS *BATMAN* FLAPTRAP, WELL...

...IT'S NOISY, ALL RIGHT. THAT BIG *CAPE* AND POINTY *EARS* -- IT'S GREAT *SHOW BIZ.* AND YOU KNOW THE *PRESIDENT* KNOWS HIS *SHOW BIZ.* YOU JUST KEEP YOUR *SHORTS* ON, TED...

...PRETTY SOON NOW THE *RATINGS'LL* DROP ON THIS ONE AND IT'LL BLOW *OVER.* BESIDES, I THINK THE WHOLE THING'S JUST AS LIKELY A *HOAX.* NETWORKS'VE DONE *WORSE.*

I MEAN, BATBOY'D BE PUSHING *SIXTY* BY NOW-- IF HE EVER WAS REAL. FUNNY NOBODY'S EVER TAKEN A *PICTURE* OF HIM... *MIGHTY* FUNNY, I SAY...

MISS LANG, YOU ARE THE BATMAN'S MOST *VOCAL* SUPPORTER. HOW CAN YOU CONDONE BEHAVIOR THAT'S SO BLATANTLY *ILLEGAL?* WHAT ABOUT *DUE PROCESS--CIVIL RIGHTS?*

WE LIVE IN THE *SHADOW* OF CRIME, TED, WITH THE UNSPOKEN UNDERSTANDING THAT WE ARE *VICTIMS*--OF *FEAR, OF VIOLENCE,* OF SOCIAL *IMPOTENCE.*

A *MAN* HAS RISEN TO SHOW US THAT THE POWER IS, AND ALWAYS HAS BEEN, IN *OUR* HANDS. WE ARE UNDER *SIEGE* -- HE'S SHOWING US THAT WE CAN *RESIST.*

IT'S THE *TRAIN*, THINKS MARGARET CORCORAN. MY LEGS NEVER HURT LIKE THIS WHEN I WAIT THE TABLES.

THE *TRAIN*-- IT WON'T LET THE PAIN LIE IN MY *CALVES* WHERE I'M *USED* TO IT.

VARICOSE VEINS, THE DOCTOR SAID. EASY FOR HIM TO TELL HER TO QUIT HER JOB. EASY FOR *HIM* TO TALK ABOUT *SURGERY*.

SURGERY. WITH NO INSURANCE AND TWO PAYMENTS LEFT ON JAMIE'S BRACES AND THE TURN-OFF NOTICE FROM THE ELECTRIC COMPANY WITH WINTER ON ITS WAY.

SHE FEELS THE METAL SQUARE INSIDE HER PURSE AND SMILES.

ALMOST NOBODY TIPS ANYMORE. BUT AN UPTOWN DRUNK LEFT TEN DOLLARS ON THE TABLE TONIGHT. WHAT WITH THE TURN-OFF NOTICE IT WAS WRONG TO SPEND THE TIP ON THE PAIN.

BUT YOUNG ROBERT'S *ART TEACHER* SAYS HE HAS *TALENT*...

SHE PICTURES ROBERT'S ABLE LITTLE HANDS, HIS EAGER SMILE...

HER *PURSE STRAP* BITES INTO HER SHOULDER...

...AND MARGARET CORCORAN, WHO HAD NOT PLEADED WITH BLUE CROSS WHEN THEY CANCELLED HER INSURANCE OR WITH *CITICORP* WHEN THEY REPOSSESSED HER CAR...

...BEGS LIKE A WINO FOR A TEN-DOLLAR PAINT SET.

SHE FEELS HER PURSE HIT HER STOMACH AS THE TRAIN RUMBLES TO A STOP. SHE HEARS THEM LAUGH.

SHE LANDS HARD ON THE CEMENT, BUT IT ONLY HURTS.

SHE FEELS THE SQUARE OF METAL AND THANKS GOD AND CAN'T HELP BUT CRY.

THEN SHE FEELS SOMETHING HEAVY AND ROUND LIKE AN APPLE IN HER PURSE...

WOMAN EXPLODES IN SUBWAY STATION-- FILM AT ELEVEN.

THE GENERAL'S RECORD
IS AN *ANTHEM* OF
ORDERS BARKED
BETWEEN DEAFENING
EXPLOSIONS... OF A
STEELY, REASSURING
VOICE ABOVE THE
CRIES OF WOUNDED
MEN...

...AN ANTHEM,
SHATTERED INTO
DISCORD IN ITS
LAST FEW NOTES--
BY MISAPPROPRIATED
WEAPONS...SOLD
TO THE MUTANTS.

I ALMOST
ASKED
HIM WHY...

BLACK'S *PASSÉ*, YOUR HONOR. BESIDES, DALE'S *NEUTRAL* ON THE *BATMAN* THING. AND YOU KNOW WHAT YOUR OWN *NEUTRALITY* IS COSTING YOU...

I'M NOT *NEUTRAL*. WHO SAYS I'M *NEUTRAL*? I'M *CONFLICTED*.

SEEMS TO ME THAT THIS IS YOUR BIG *CHANCE*, YOUR HONOR.-- TO SHOW WHAT A *LEADER* YOU ARE -- TO MAKE A *BOLD DECISION* ABOUT BATMAN...

DECISIONS-- YOU'D THINK ALL THERE IS TO RUNNING A CITY IS MAKING *DECISIONS*...

WELL, ALL *RIGHT*, GALLAGHER-- I'LL MAKE A *DECISION*. I'LL *SHOW* THEM WHO'S BOSS. ON MY OWN PRIVATE *AUTHORITY*-- --I ASSIGN YOU THE TASK OF FINDING ME A POLICE COMMISSIONER.

I ALREADY *HAVE*, SIR.

MASTER BRUCE?

WHO *ELSE*, ALFRED?

OF COURSE, SIR. IT'S JUST THAT THE SIGNAL IS COMING FROM INSIDE THE--

THAT'S *RIGHT*, ALFRED, I'M TAKING HER *OUT*.

I HIT THE *ENGINE*. SHE RESPONDS LIKE IT WAS *YESTERDAY*.

IT *IS* YESTERDAY...

I AM EXCITED--NO, *THRILLED*-CAN'T YOU TELL I'M THRILLED?-- TO GIVE YOU THE NEXT *POLICE COMMISSIONER* OF GOTHAM CITY...

...CAPTAIN ELLEN YINDEL.

THE *YOUNGEST* EVER TO HOLD THE OFFICE--AND, OF COURSE, THE FIRST *WOMAN*-- ELLEN YINDEL BRINGS WITH HER AN *ASTONISHING* ARREST RECORD FROM CHICAGO. SHE WAS QUICK TO ANSWER ON THE SUBJECT OF *BATMAN*...

I'M SURPRISED THERE *IS* A CONTROVERSY. HIS ACTIONS ARE CATEGORICALLY *CRIMINAL*. I WILL HAVE HIM BROUGHT TO TRIAL. EXCUSE ME?...

...YES. I'LL BE SPECIFIC. MY FIRST ACT AS *POLICE COMMISSIONER* WILL BE TO ISSUE AN *ARREST WARRANT* FOR THE BATMAN ON CHARGES OF *ASSAULT, BREAKING AND ENTERING, CREATING A PUBLIC HAZARD*...

LITTLE MORE THAN *HALF* THE AGE OF THE MAN SHE'S *REPLACING*, ELLEN YINDEL IS--

A WOMAN. CHRIST ALMIGHTY...

KLK

DID YOU SAY SOMETHING, JIM?

...NOTHING, SWEETHEART...

THE *DUMP* STRETCHES OUT OF SIGHT FROM THE FAR BANK OF THE *WEST RIVER.* I'M TOLD IT ENDS SOMEWHERE BEFORE THE *FARMLANDS.*

IT SMELLS OF *ROT* AND *RUST--* IT'S A BREEDING GROUND FOR *INSECTS* AND *RODENTS.*

I CUT THE ENGINE AND LISTEN TO ONE OF THE RODENTS.

THEY CALL US A *GANG.* THEY CALL US A *MOB.* THEY THINK WE JUST *NOISY KIDS.*

ONLY WHEN THEY *DIE* BY OUR *HANDS* AND SEE THEIR WOMEN *RAPED* WILL THEY KNOW...

--WE HAVE THE *STRENGTH--* WE HAVE THE *WILL--* AND NOW WE HAVE THE *GUNS.*

GOTHAM CITY BELONGS TO THE *MUTANTS!*

TAKE THE GUNS. *TAKE* THE BOMBS. STORM POLICE HEADQUARTERS.

KILL AND *KILL.*

BRING ME THE *HEAD* OF THE *OLD MAN GORDON.*

MY *TRUNCHEON* WILL CARRY IT THROUGH THE STREETS.

I LISTEN FOR AS LONG AS I CAN STOMACH IT...

...THEN I LET THEM KNOW I'M HERE.

I SHALL *CRUSH* THE FOOL--

CHIK

--BATMA *AAA*

B OO M

I MODIFIED HER DURING
SOME NASTY RIOTS
FIFTEEN YEARS AGO. THE
ONLY THING I KNOW OF
THAT CAN CUT THROUGH
HER HIDE ISN'T FROM
THIS PLANET.

THE MUTANTS USE HAND GRENADES.
THEY USE ROCKET LAUNCHERS.
SOMETHING BOUNCES OFF THE
HULL THAT MUST HAVE COME FROM
A BAZOOKA.

THEY DO EACH OTHER
A LOT OF DAMAGE.

AAARRR

MFF

KLUDD

KRAMP

I MAKE HIM EAT SOME GARBAGE--

--THEN I HELP HIM SWALLOW IT.

THWAKK

A BEAUTY TO HIS SOLAR PLEXIS -- I WORRY HE MIGHT DROP TOO SOON--

--THEN HIS CLAWS DIG INTO MY BACK--

GGGRAAAAAAAA

--HIS FILED TEETH LIKE RAZORS IN MY TRAPEZIUS--

CHUD

FAPP

HA! YOU SLOW, MAN!

HE'S RIGHT-- HE HAD ALL THE TIME IN THE WORLD--

--HE SHOWS ME WHAT A FAST KICK IS--

WHUKK

--SOMETHING EXPLODES IN MY MIDSECTION--

--SUNLIGHT BEHIND MY EYES AS THE PAIN RISES--

--A MOMENT OF *BLACKNESS*-- TOO SOON FOR THAT--

--TOO *SOON*-- WHAT'S WRONG WITH ME--

NO--

--RIBS INTACT--

--NO INTERNAL BLEEDING--

--LET IT LOOK WORSE THAN IT IS--

--LET HIM-- GET *CLOSE*--

--NOT YET--

--NOT YET--

-- GIVE HIM-- EVERYTHING I'VE GOT--

--HIS NECK --HOLDS--

--HIS NOSE-- SHATTERS--

--BONE BITES INTO MY KNUCKLES--

--THE IDIOT--

--STARTS LAUGHING--

LUCKY...YOU'RE LUCKY I'M ALWAYS HERE...

...TO BAIL YOU OUT...

...DICK...

STILL ALIVE--

PORN STAR **HOT GATES** TODAY SIGNED A TWELVE-MILLION-DOLLAR CONTRACT WITH **LANDMARK FILMS** TO STAR IN A SCREEN VERSION OF **SNOW WHITE.** "I'M DOING IT FOR THE KIDS," SAYS GATES...

IN OTHER NEWS, GALAXY BROADCASTING PRESIDENT JAMES OLSEN ASSURED VIEWERS THAT THE TELEVISION WRITERS' STRIKE, NOW IN ITS FOURTH YEAR, WILL NOT AFFECT THE YEAR'S PROGRAMMING...

...THE **POLITICAL PERFORMANCE COMMISSION** HAS AWARDED THE **PRESIDENT** AN UNPRECEDENTED **FIVE CREDIBILITY POINTS** FOR HIS HANDLING OF PUBLIC PERCEPTION DURING THE ECONOMIC CRISIS...

...THIS JUST IN--EYEWITNESSES REPORT EXPLOSIONS RIPPING ACROSS THE **GOTHAM DUMP.** A NEWS FOUR **HELICOPTER** IS ON ITS WAY, FOLKS...

GENTLY, NOW. GENTLY, GOOD GIRL.

NOW YOU JUST RUN ALONG HOME...

SON, I HOPE YOU DON'T MIND IF I GET RIGHT DOWN TO BRASS TACKS...

NOT AT ALL, MR. PRESIDENT, YOUR TIME IS PRECIOUS.

GUESS IT IS AT THAT...

...WELL, SON, YOU KNOW I LIKE TO KEEP YOU OUT OF DOMESTIC AFFAIRS...WHAT WITH ALL THE RUCKUS YOU KICK UP.

YES, SIR.

WELL, IT'S A RUCKUS I'D LIKE YOU TO STRAIGHTEN OUT FOR ME -- IN GOTHAM CITY. JUST BETWEEN YOU AND ME AND THE FENCE POST, I'M WORRIED... ABOUT A FRIEND OF YOURS.

HERE... HAVE A MINT.

THANK YOU, SIR, BUT I'M NOT HUNGRY.

I LOVE MINTS...

SON, I LIKE TO THINK I LEARNED EVERYTHING I KNOW ABOUT RUNNING THIS COUNTRY ON MY RANCH...I KNOW IT'S CORNY, BUT I LIKE TO THINK IT...

...AND, WELL, IT'S ALL WELL AND GOOD... ON A RANCH, I MEAN ...FOR THE HORSES TO BE ALL DIFFERENT COLORS AND SIZES... LONG AS THEY STAY INSIDE THE FENCE...

...IT'S EVEN OKAY TO HAVE A CRAZY BRONCO NOW AND THEN... DOES THE HANDS GOOD TO BREAK HIM IN...

...BUT IF THAT BRONCO UP AND KICKS THE FENCE OUT AND GETS THE OTHER HORSES CRAZY...WELL, IT'S BAD FOR BUSINESS.

WORLD'S CHANGED, SON, IT'S NOT LIKE THE OLD DAYS. I WISH IT WERE. I'D GIVE HIM A MEDAL. YOU WANT A MEDAL, SON?

NO, THANK YOU, SIR.

I LOVE MEDALS...

...NOW, SON, I'M NOT ASKING YOU TO DRAG HIM KICKING AND SCREAMING INTO THE STABLE. JUST SETTLE HIM DOWN... RIDE HIM AROUND THE YARD A FEW TIMES IF YOU HAVE TO...

SIR, I CAN TALK TO HIM, BUT--

WELL, I'D SURE APPRECIATE IT... I'D JUST HATE TO SEE THINGS GET OUT OF...WELL, I'D JUST HATE THAT.

GIVE IT A SHOT, SON, YOUR COUNTRY'S COUNTING ON YOU...

...YES, SIR.

GOOD BOY...

OH, DEAR ...HE'S NOT DOING WELL AT ALL...

PLEASE, DEAR--STAY OUT OF THE WAY OF THE SENSOR.

WHAT ARE YOU DOING WITH HIS ARM, YOUNG LADY?

...A SCENE OF TOTAL WARFARE! EIGHTY-THREE MEMBERS OF THE MUTANT GANG HAVE BEEN FOUND, SUFFERING FROM BULLET AND SHRAPNEL WOUNDS.

AMONG THOSE CAPTURED BY POLICE IS THE MUTANT LEADER, WHO CLAIMS THE BATMAN USED MILITARY WEAPONS IN THE ATTACK--AND ALSO CLAIMS TO HAVE DEFEATED THE BATMAN IN PERSONAL COMBAT...

BATMAN IS A **COWARD**. I **BROKE** HIS BONES. I **CONQUERED** THE FOOL. I MADE HIM **BEG** FOR MERCY. ONLY BY **CHEATING** DID HE ESCAPE ALIVE.

LET HIM GO TO HIS **WOMEN**. LET HIM **LICK** HIS WOUNDS. HIS DAY IS **DONE**. GOTHAM CITY BELONGS TO THE **MUTANTS**.

CAREFUL, MAN--YOU'RE BOUNCING AROUND TOO--

NO... ...NOT... BOUNCING ME...DON'T WORRY...

SKREECH

STRETCHER'S... ON A GYROSCOPE... STAYS LEVEL... NO MATTER WHAT...

THAT'S KEEN.

NOW DON'T YOU **STRAIN** YOURSELF, SIR. YOU'VE QUITE A LOT OF INTERNAL BLEEDING.

THIS YOUNG LADY WAS KIND ENOUGH TO HELP YOU ABOARD...

I...KNOW WHAT SHE DID, ALFRED.

WHERE...DID YOU LEARN TO SET AN **ARM**... MAKE A **SPLINT**...?

GIRL SCOUTS.

WHAT'S... YOUR **NAME**...

CARRIE. CARRIE KELLEY.

ROBIN.

MINE'S BRUCE...

SIR! YOU'RE **DELIRIOUS**, SIR. YOU JUST **REST** NOW--DON'T TRY TO **SPEAK**--

WE'RE ONLY **MOMENTS** FROM THE HOSPITAL--

NO... HOSPITAL, ALFRED...

...THE **CAVE**...

BUT SIR--

THE **CAVE**...

...AND **ROBIN**... COMES WITH US...

SOON MY ARMY WILL **STORM** GOTHAM CITY. SOON THE HEAD OF **GORDON** WILL BE CARRIED THROUGH THE **STREETS**. THEN I WILL HUNT YOUR **NEW** COP--YOUR **WOMAN** COP--AND I WILL

THE REST OF
THE MUTANT LEADER'S
STATEMENT IS
UNFIT FOR
BROADCAST.

I DON'T
THINK YOU
REALIZE
WHAT YOU'RE
SUGGESTING,
DR. WOLPER...

HARVEY DENT
DIDN'T EXACTLY
BRING US
POSITIVE
PUBLICITY.
AND THIS
ONE...

I KNOW,
GLEN. I
KNOW--

ARKHAM
• HOME •
FOR THE
EMOTIONALLY TROUBLED

--BUT I'M NOT
TALKING ABOUT
A RELEASE. THIS
WILL BE A
CONTROLLED
ENVIRONMENT--
AND IT WOULD
BE SO GOOD
FOR HIM.

HIM
I'M NOT
WORRIED
ABOUT.

DR. GLEN F
CHIEF ADM

COME NOW, GLEN!
HE'S BEEN
NEARLY COMATOSE
FOR MORE THAN
A DECADE. IF
YOU'D JUST
TALK WITH HIM...
FOR FIVE
MINUTES,
GLEN...

I DON'T
KNOW.
THERE'S
SOMETHING
...WELL...
SOMETHING
SUPERNATURAL
ABOUT
THAT ONE.

HIEF ADMINIS

NOW THAT'S A FINE WAY TO
SPEAK IN A HOUSE OF MEDICINE,
ISN'T IT? LISTEN-- PUT ALL
THE GUARDS YOU WANT IN THE
STUDIO, IF IT WILL MAKE YOU
FEEL BETTER.

FIVE MINUTES,
GLEN. HE IS A
PATIENT.

LEN FORB
ADMINISTRATOR

OKAY. ALL
RIGHT.
FIVE
MINUTES.

'SCUSE ME, WE'RE
HEADING STRAIGHT
FOR A BRICK
WALL.

DON'T...
WORRY,
ROBIN...

...IT'S JUST
...A
HOLOGRAM...

SIR--I URGE YOU TO REJECT
DR. WOLPER'S SUGGESTION.
I DON'T DESERVE THIS
CHARITY... MY CRIMES...WERE
HORRIBLE BEYOND
ALL WORDS... I AM
BEYOND
REDEMPTION.

PLEASE--JUST
LOCK ME AWAY--
FROM HUMAN
MEMORY...

SOB

GLIDING WITH *ANCIENT* GRACE...

EYES *GLEAMING,* UNTOUCHED BY LOVE OR JOY OR SORROW...

BREATH HOT WITH THE TASTE OF FALLEN FOES... THE STENCH OF DEAD THINGS, *DAMNED* THINGS...

SURELY THE FIERCEST SURVIVOR ...THE *PUREST* WARRIOR...

GLARING, *HATING...*

...CLAIMING ME AS YOUR *OWN.*

WE WILL COME FOR OUR LEADER. WE WILL *RAZE* GOTHAM. WE WILL *RAPE* GOTHAM. WE WILL TASTE GOTHAM'S *BLOOD.*

ON HEARING THIS MESSAGE FROM THE MUTANTS, COMMISSIONER GORDON PUT HIMSELF AND HIS MEN ON TWENTY-FOUR HOUR ALERT--WHILE THE MAYOR WAS QUICK TO SPEAK OUT...

THIS WHOLE SITUATION IS THE RESULT OF GORDON'S *INCOMPETENCE*--AND OF THE TERRORIST ACTIONS OF THE *BATMAN.* I WISH TO SIT DOWN WITH THE MUTANT LEADER...TO NEGOTIATE A *SETTLEMENT...*

WHAT DO YOU THINK, TRISH? HIS HONOR GONE *NUTS?*

NOT AT ALL, BILL. FRANKLY I EXPECT THE MAYOR'S CREDIBILITY RATING TO GO THROUGH THE *ROOF,* *ESPECIALLY* IF HE'S *SUCCESSFUL* IN THE NEGOTIATIONS.

THIS, COMBINED WITH HIS STRONG STAND ON *BATMAN*-- AND MAKING A WOMAN THE NEXT POLICE COMMISSIONER-- WELL, I THINK WE'VE GOT A WHOLE NEW *MAYOR* ON OUR HANDS--

--PUBLIC PERCEPTION- WISE, THAT IS.

ALL THIS AND BRAINS TOO!

ARNOLD CRIMP FINGERS THE COLD STEEL THING IN HIS POCKET AND STARES AT THE MOVIE MARQUEE AND DOES NOT THROW UP.

HE THINKS ABOUT **LED ZEPPELIN** AND HOW THEY ARE TRYING TO KILL HIM.

HE HAD NOT KNOWN ABOUT **LED ZEPPELIN** UNTIL **FATHER DON** ON TV HAD EXPLAINED IT LAST NIGHT.

FATHER DON SAID THAT **LED ZEPPELIN** HID A PRAYER TO **SATAN** IN THEIR SONG "STAIRWAY TO HEAVEN."

THEY HID IT VERY WELL. THEY RECORDED IT **BACKWARDS**.

ARNOLD CRIMP TOOK THE ALBUM FROM THE RECORD STORE **WHERE HE WORKED UNTIL THEY FIRED HIM THIS AFTERNOON** AND TRANSFERRED "STAIRWAY TO HEAVEN" TO TAPE.

THEN HE PLAYED THE TAPE BACKWARDS.

HE PLAYED IT FORTY-SEVEN TIMES UNTIL HE WAS ABSOLUTELY CERTAIN THAT FATHER DON WAS RIGHT.

BUT THE YOUNG GIRL WHO WAS PAINTED LIKE A WHORE DIDN'T BELIEVE HIM.

THAT WAS THIS AFTERNOON, IN THE STORE. HE EXPLAINED IT TO HER VERY CAREFULLY. SHE SAID AWFUL WORDS.

HE LOST HIS TEMPER AND BROKE THE RECORD INTO FOUR PIECES THAT WERE EXACTLY THE SAME SIZE.

THE YOUNG GIRL **WHO WAS PAINTED JUST LIKE A WHORE** SCREAMED FOR THE MANAGER AND THE MANAGER WALKED OUT FROM THE BACK ROOM AND WOULDN'T EVEN LISTEN AND FIRED ARNOLD CRIMP,

THAT WAS THIS AFTERNOON, IN THE STORE.

EVERY MORNING AND EVENING **UNTIL TONIGHT OF COURSE** HE HAD WALKED SIX BLOCKS OUT OF HIS WAY TO AVOID THIS NEIGHBORHOOD.

IT'S WORSE THAN HE IMAGINED,

ROW ON ROW ON ROW ON ROW OF PICTURES OF WOMEN AND **WORDS** AND **WORDS** AND **WORDS**. HE STOPPED AT THIS ONE **THE ONE HE IS IN RIGHT NOW** AND READ THE TITLE THAT DID NOT MAKE HIM THROW UP.

THE TITLE IS "MY SWEET SATAN," WHICH IS WHAT ARNOLD CRIMP IS ABSOLUTELY CERTAIN HE HEARD WHEN HE PLAYED "STAIRWAY TO HEAVEN" BACKWARDS.

ON THE SCREEN A NUN A NUN IS **DOING SOMETHING** AND SHE'S PAINTED EXACTLY LIKE A **WHORE**--

THREE SLAIN IN **BATMAN**-INSPIRED PORN THEATER SHOOT-OUT. DETAILS TO FOLLOW...

IRON MAN VASQUEZ CAN'T TASTE HIS **SNICKERS** BAR.

HE KNOWS HE SHOULD BE OUT OF HERE, OUT AND HOME, WAITING FOR BIGGERS TO SEND THE SIXTY DOLLARS. THIRTY FOR EACH LEG, HE THINKS, FEELING NOTHING.

FEELING NOTHING AND NOT TASTING HIS SNICKERS BAR.

HE PUSHES THROUGH THE COTTON IN HIS HEAD AND REMEMBERS THE LAST TIME HE FELT SOMETHING.

IT WAS IN THE FIRST AND ONLY ROUND OF HIS LAST FIGHT. HIS LAST FIGHT WHEN **CAPTAIN WARRIOR** HIT HIM ACROSS THE NOSE.

BROKEN NOSE VASQUEZ, BIGGERS HAD CALLED HIM. JUST **LAUGHED** WHEN IRON MAN CRIED LIKE A **BABY** AND BEGGED FOR ANOTHER FIGHT.

THEN BIGGERS PUT HIS FAT ARM AROUND IRON MAN'S SHOULDER AND TOLD HIM THE ONLY WAY HE COULD MAKE MONEY NOW.

SUDDENLY HIS EYES STING AND IRON MAN HURTS ALL OVER AND REALIZES HE'S READING ABOUT A **MAN.**

A MAN WHO DRESSES UP LIKE A MONSTER AND MAKES THINGS RIGHT.

THE NEXT TIME IRON MAN VASQUEZ FEELS SOMETHING, HE'S STANDING IN A RESTAURANT WITH SOMETHING ON HIS FACE AND A GUN IN HIS HAND.

HE HEARS A TRUCK BACKFIRE--

CRAZED WOULD-BE KILLER DRESSES AS **BATMAN--** AFTER THIS...

A DEVOUT CATHOLIC, PEPPI SPANDECK CAN'T SAY HE **APPROVES** OF THIS **BATMAN.**

AND WHEN HE HEARS THE WOMAN **SCREAM** DOWN THE STREET, HE KNOWS HE SHOULD BE **AFRAID.**

INSTEAD HE'S LOOKING AT THE ALARM SYSTEM THAT COST HIM TWO MONTHS' **PROFITS** AND THE IRON BARS OVER HIS WINDOWS THAT MAKE HIS BEAUTIFUL SHOP LOOK LIKE A PRISON...

HE CAN FEEL HIS PULSE, JUST BELOW HIS EARS. HE KNOWS HE'S GONE CRAZY. BUT THE MUGGER IS RUNNING, AFRAID. AFRAID OF PEPPI.

NOBODY IS HURT BADLY ENOUGH FOR THIS TO MAKE THE NEWS.

...AN **UPDATE**--THE **MAYOR** IS THIS MINUTE **IN CONSULTATION** WITH THE MUTANT **LEADER**, WHO HAS AGREED TO MEET HIM **ALONE**. MEANWHILE, THE MAYOR'S **LEADERSHIP QUOTIENT** HAS **SOARED**-- EXCUSE ME...

I'D EXPECTED THEM TO BE **SCREAMING** AND **FIGHTING**. BUT THEY STAND LIKE A CAPTIVE ARMY. I'D LIKE TO THINK THEY'RE **CRAZY**-- BUT HERE I AM, WALKING THE **MAYOR** TO MEET THEIR **LEADER**--

-- WITH ALL THE **CEREMONY** OF A MILITARY **CONFERENCE**.

THE CELL DOOR **OPENS**. THE AIR GOES **THICK**. I FEEL THE MAYOR **SHUDDER**, IN TIME WITH ME.

I ASK HIM ONE MORE TIME IF HE IS SURE HE WANTS TO GO IT ALONE. HE GURGLES, AND NODS.

I DON'T KNOW IF I'D CALL IT **COURAGE**.

I HEAR A NERVOUS **GIGGLE** AND AN ANIMAL **GROWL**. I HEAR HANDCUFF LINKS **SNAP**.

I SEE SOMETHING I'LL TAKE TO MY **GRAVE**.

SOME IDIOT STOPS ME FROM DOING THE **OBVIOUS** THING.

...THE MAYOR IS DEAD.

THE MUTANT LEADER RIPPED THE MAYOR'S THROAT OUT WITH HIS TEETH. THE MUTANT HAS BEEN RETURNED TO HIS CELL. MORE ON THIS AS WE GET IT.

THAT'S **RIGHT**--WE'VE GOT **POLICE VIDEOTAPE** OF THE **MAYOR'S MURDER!** ONLY ON CHANNEL **TWO!** **NOT** FOR THE **SQUEAMISH.** STAY TUNED.

SOVIET DESTROYERS HAVE BEEN SIGHTED IN THE WATERS OFF **CORTO MALTESE...**

AND, IN **GOTHAM CITY,** IT **ALSO** LOOKS LIKE IMPENDING WAR-- AS THE CITY **GIRDS** ITSELF FOR THE MUTANT **ATTACK...**

CHECK WHAT'S COMIN, MAN-- SOME PIECE--

TASTY-- HEY-- IS THAT WHO I THINK-- IT IS--

HEY, SWEET PIECE--WE GOT PLANS F YOU--

NIZE PLANS.

FRIGID BITCH--

WE CURE HER...

A FRIGHTENED **SILENCE** HAS FALLEN OVER GOTHAM. SILENCE BROKEN ONLY BY THE URGENT WORDS OF DEPUTY MAYOR-- EXCUSE ME-- **MAYOR** STEVENSON...

IF THERE ARE ANY MEMBERS OF THE **MUTANT ORGANIZATION** LISTENING, PLEASE--PLEASE-- WE ARE STILL OPEN TO NEGOTIATION...

YOU'VE BEEN THROUGH QUITE A **LOT,** MASTER BRUCE. IT FOLLOWS THAT YOUR JUDGMENT MAY BE **IMPAIRED.**

WHAT ARE YOU GETTING AT, ALFRED?

IT'S THE GIRL, SIR.

CARRIE. SHE'S PERFECT.

SHE'S **YOUNG.** SHE'S **SMART.** SHE'S **BRAVE.**

WITH HER, I MIGHT BE ABLE TO END THIS MUTANT NONSENSE ONCE AND FOR ALL.

YOU SEE, IT ALL GETS DOWN TO THEIR LEADER. THEY WORSHIP HIM...

SHE'S A SWEET YOUNG CHILD.

SHE'S MORE THAN THAT.

VERY WELL, SIR. I SHALL COME RIGHT OUT WITH IT.

HAVE YOU **FORGOTTEN** WHAT HAPPENED TO JASON?

I WILL **NEVER** FORGET JASON. HE WAS A GOOD SOLDIER. HE **HONORED** ME.

BUT THE WAR GOES ON.

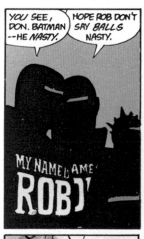

YOU SEE, DON. BATMAN --HE *NASTY*.

HOPE ROB DON'T SAY *BALLS* NASTY.

BALLS NASTY.

SHH!

HE'S FAST--FASTER THAN I AM. AND STRONGER--

--AND SEEMINGLY IMPERVIOUS TO PAIN.

BUT THEY DO COME SMARTER.

--AND NOBODY'S VERY FAST WHEN HE'S THIGH-DEEP IN MUD.

I WAIT FOR HIM TO TRY A KICK--

-- GIVE HIM JUST THE *RIGHT* KIND OF CUT ABOVE THE EYES.

THE KIND THAT BLEEDS.

MY MISTAKE WAS TO TRY TO MATCH HIS SAVAGERY.

TO FIGHT LIKE A *YOUNG* MAN.

RIGHT ON *SCHEDULE* THE BLOOD HITS HIS EYES.

I GRAB A CLUMP OF MUD.

SPLOOT

LEADER'S BOGGIN'!

LEADER BILLY BERSERK, SPUD. LEADER PEG BATMAN. YOU SEE.

SHH!

HE CHARGES, BLIND --

--A QUICK ONE TO THE NERVE CLUSTER IN HIS *DELTOID*. IT DOESN'T HURT HIM --

-- BUT NO FORCE ON EARTH COULD HELP HIM MOVE HIS *LEFT ARM* NOW.

HIS *RIGHT*--

--IT'S FAST--

--TOO FAST--

HE DUSTED! HE DUSTED!

MY MON BATS DON'T SHIV.

YOU SEE.

BLACKNESS--
COMES IN FROM
THE EDGES--

I GET SICK OF
THE ARM--

--AND KILL
IT BELOW
THE ELBOW.

HE SPINS--AT
THE PERFECT
MOMENT--

--GOES FOR
MY THROAT--

--HAVE TO--
TAKE US
DOWN--

YOU DON'T
...GET IT,
BOY...
THIS ISN'T
A MUDHOLE...

...IT'S AN
OPERATING
TABLE.

AND I'M THE
SURGEON.

SOMETHING
TELLS ME
TO STOP
WITH THE
LEG.

I DON'T
LISTEN
TO IT.

THE MUTANTS ARE **DEAD**. THE MUTANTS ARE **HISTORY**. THIS IS THE MARK OF THE **FUTURE**. **GOTHAM CITY** BELONGS TO THE **BATMAN**.

JUST AS I PREDICTED--THE BATMAN HAS **INFECTED** THE YOUTH OF GOTHAM-- **POISONED** THEM WITH AN INSIDIOUS **EXCUSE** FOR THE MOST VIOLENTLY ANTI-SOCIAL BEHAVIOR.

WE'RE NOT TALKING ABOUT LETTING THE MUTANT LEADER GO. ONCE HE IS **MOBILE** HE WILL BE **ARRAIGNED**-- TO SEE IF HE IS FIT TO STAND TRIAL, OR THE **VICTIM** OF **MENTAL ILLNESS.**

BATMAN? I'M PLAIN TIRED OF **HEARING** ABOUT HIM. HIM AND HOW HE DOESN'T LET THINGS **STOP** HIM OR JUST LET THINGS **GO** THE WAY US **HUMANS** DO. WE COUNT **TOO.**

THOUGH SURROUNDED BY SINFULNESS AND **TERROR**, WE MUST NOT BECOME SO **EMBITTERED** THAT WE TAKE SATAN'S METHODS AS OUR OWN.

DO NOT **EXPECT** ANY FURTHER **STATEMENTS**. THE **SONS** OF THE **BATMAN** DO NOT **TALK**. WE **ACT**. LET GOTHAM'S **CRIMINALS BEWARE**. THEY ARE ABOUT TO ENTER **HELL.**

SO A BUNCH OF **PSYCHOPATHS** TURN ON **CRIMINALS**, INSTEAD OF INNOCENTS. FOR THIS YOU WANT TO **BLAME** BATMAN?

THE PRESIDENT IS CONCERNED, YOU CAN **BANK** ON THAT, PAL. BUT DON'T EXPECT HIM TO GO JUMPING IN ON GOTHAM'S OWN FINE MAYOR AND GOVERNOR. NO, SIR. THIS IS **AMERICA.**

I SAID **NO COMMENT.**

LET ME TELL YOU MY *SECRET.*

SEEMS EVERYBODY WANTS TO KNOW WHAT IT IS.

...THEY TELL ME I'M HANDLING IT *WELL*-- MY *RETIREMENT,* THAT IS -- THEY *SMILE* AND *STARE* AT ME, A LITTLE TOO *OBVIOUS* ABOUT HOW *CURIOUS* THEY ARE.

ELLEN YINDEL
COMMISSIONER OF POLICE

THEY WONDER HOW I CAN LEAVE IT *BEHIND* WITHOUT AT LEAST A MONTH OR TWO OF FEELING *USELESS.*

ELLEN YINDEL
COMMISSIONER OF POLICE

FIFTY YEARS OF *THIS* AND THEY *WONDER.*

LIFE WILL BE EASIER NOW. I WON'T FEEL LIKE *DAD* TO AN ENTIRE CITY OF SOULS. I WON'T *BLEED* WITH EVERY SINGLE ONE OF MY *CHILDREN.*

WHEN I THINK OF *BRUCE*--AND WHAT HE'S IN FOR...I DON'T THINK HE CAN POSSIBLY KNOW HOW MUCH I BENT AND BROKE THE RULES FOR HIM, ALL THESE YEARS...

...WHEN I THINK OF BRUCE-- THEN, I WISH THEY *HADN'T* RETIRED ME. HE'S *FINISHED.* AND THERE'S NO WAY TO TELL HIM THAT.

AND NO *POINT,* I GUESS.

I WON'T BE SEEING HIM AGAIN. I MEAN, SURE, I'LL *SEE* HIM--HE'S THAT CLOSE TO POLITE, BUT I'M OUT OF THE PICTURE NOW. OUT OF HIS PICTURE.

I WAS GOING TO TELL YOU MY *SECRET.* THE ONE I'LL TELL NOBODY AT THE BANQUET--

--GOD, WHAT WILL I SAY AT THE *BANQUET?*--

--IT'S A *SIMPLE* SECRET.

I THINK OF *SARAH.*

THE REST IS *EASY.*

THE WIND *RISES,* TEARING *DEAD* LEAVES FREE.

FROGS CROAK LIKE A CARTOON CAR ALARM. CRICKETS PICK UP THE CHORUS.

A WOLF HOWLS.

I KNOW HOW HE FEELS.

HUNT THE DARK KNIGHT

BRUCE, YOU IDIOT.

YOU'LL RUIN EVERYTHING.

FOR ALL OF US.

I ALWAYS KNEW YOU WOULD...

I'VE WAITED LONG *ENOUGH*, YOU SOFT GLOB OF *SNOT*.

EMPTY THE *CASH REGISTER*-- OR MY *BULLETS* WILL TEAR THROUGH YOUR *BRAIN*, BREAKING IT INTO MOIST, GOOEY *LUMPS*...

THAT'S IF I DON'T GIVE WITH A *SURPRISE* FROM UP THE *SLEEVE*, HUH, *BRUNO*?

CLERK GONE *BILLY*, ROB.

BRUNO GET *NASTY*, DON, *YOU* SEE.

BRUNO DON'T *SHIV*.

YOUR *BOYS*--USED TO BE *MUTANTS*, HUH? GUESS SINCE THEIR *BOSS* GOT HIS *ASS* FLATTENED THEY'LL WORK FOR *ANYBODY*.

GUESS WITH YOUR *BOYFRIEND* IN THE LOONY BIN YOU GOT TO PAY FOR YOUR OWN *BODYWORK*.

NICE WORK, TOO. CAN BARELY SEE THE *STRETCH MARKS*.

I'LL STRIP YOUR FLESH WITH MY *TEETH*...

THIEF! YOU'RE A THIEF!

SEBBIN LEBBIN SELLS THIS FOR *TWO-FIFTY!*

BRUNO IS COMING YOUR *WAY*, ROBIN.

GET HER INTO THE ALLEY. DO NOT LET HER *SEE* YOU.

BOYS, BOYS, BOYS... ONE AT A TIME NOW... NOW HOW ABOUT THAT SMARTLY DRESSED YOUNGSTER IN THE *FRONT ROW* THERE...

MR. PRESIDENT-- WE'RE ALL ANXIOUS TO HEAR YOUR PLANS FOR THE *CORTO MALTESE CRISIS.* BUT FIRST, ANOTHER QUESTION MUCH ON THE MINDS OF AMERICA. WHAT IS YOUR *POSITION* ON THE *BATMAN* CONTROVERSY?

WELL, I DON'T THINK THAT'S MY BULL TO -- MY ROW TO HOE, BOYS...HEH... YOU SEE. THAT'S A RIGHT BIG *STATE*, ALL ITS OWN...AND IT'S GOT ITS OWN SOLID, CLEAR-HEADED GOVERNOR, YES, IT DOES...

SORRY, GUYS. I'M THE *GOVERNOR.* GOT A WHOLE *STATE* TO LOOK AFTER. I TRUST THE JUDGMENT OF THE MAYOR OF GOTHAM CITY IMPLICITLY.

AS *MAYOR,* IT IS MY DUTY TO ADMINISTRATE-- NOT TO RENDER MORAL JUDGMENTS. DON'T ASK ME TO INTERFERE WITH THE DECISION-MAKING POWER OF OUR NEW POLICE COMMISSIONER.

AND SO THE *BATMAN* BUCK IS *PASSED*-- TO ELLEN *YINDEL,* WHO REPLACES JAMES GORDON AS POLICE COMMISSIONER TONIGHT. WILL SHE FULFILL HER *PROMISE* TO ISSUE AN ARREST WARRANT FOR THE *BATMAN?*

CHANNEL TWO WILL BROADCAST THE BANQUET *LIVE.* GORDON IS SCHEDULED TO INTRODUCE YINDEL-- A GRACEFUL GESTURE, CONSIDERING THEIR DIFFERENCES. WE MAY SEE SOME SPARKS FLY. TOM?

THAT WE MAY, LOLA. WE'LL BE RIGHT BACK, AS *JULIE PARKS* BRINGS US A STORY WE DON'T KNOW WHETHER TO CLASSIFY AS AN ATMO-SPHERE ANOMALY-- OR A UFO SIGHTING.

I REPEAT. DO *NOT* LET BRUNO SEE YOU. THIS IS AN *ORDER.*

SPANG

SPUD

BRAP

NEVER MEANT-- TO GIVE HER *TIME*--

CHKCHAKK

--TO *COCK* THAT THING--

BRAPP

THIS-- WOULD BE A *STUPID* DEATH...

MISSED.

LUCKY--

--LUCKY OLD MAN...

ANOTHER *BIZARRE* INCIDENT--THIS ONE IN THE SOUTH STREET *SUBWAY STATION*. ADVERTISING AGENT *BYRON BRASSBALLS* TOLD REPORTERS...

I DIDN'T DO ANYTHING *WRONG*. I WAS JUST TRYING TO *PROTECT* MYSELF. THE SUBWAYS ARE *DANGEROUS*. YOU DON'T NEED ME TO TELL YOU THAT. SO THERE I WAS, *ALONE* IN THE STATION EXCEPT FOR THIS "*BEGGAR*"--I WANT THAT IN *QUOTES*--

--WHAT?...HOW WAS I TO KNOW HE DIDN'T HAVE A *GUN?* THEY NEVER *SHOW* YOU THAT UNTIL THEY'RE READY TO *KILL* YOU-- WHAT?...OH, *SURE*. THE *CRUTCHES*. A LOT OF THEM USE *CRUTCHES*. YOU KNOW WHAT I *MEAN*.

HEY--HE *STARTED* IT. AND IT WAS *HIS* CRUTCHES THAT TRIPPED HIM *UP*, BABE-- WHAT?...YOU *BET* HE YELLED. WANTED ME TO JUMP DOWN AND DIE *WITH* HIM. OF COURSE I *RAN*. WHO *WOULDN'T?* THEN SOMETHING HIT ME HARD--IN THE *CHEST*--

--HAVEN'T SEEN A *DOCTOR* YET, BUT I'M SURE I SLIPPED A *DISC* LANDING ON THE *TRACKS*... NO, I COULDN'T SEE. NOT A FRIGGING THING. THAT *WIND* KICKED UP TOO MUCH SOOT. SPENT A SECOND LISTENING TO THAT *BEGGAR* PRAY LIKE AN IDIOT...

...YES, I *AM* RELIGIOUS. BUT I'VE GOT THE *DECENCY* TO KEEP IT IN CHURCH. THEN I HEARD THE *SCREAM* OF TWISTING *METAL*-- *SHOUTS* FROM INSIDE THE TRAIN, PEOPLE *BITCHING*. FINALLY THE *SOOT* SETTLED...

...AND THERE IT *WAS*-- THE *TRAIN*, I MEAN-- ITS FRONT END CRUSHED INWARD, LIKE IT RAN INTO SOMETHING... WELL, SOMETHING...

SOMETHING MORE *POWERFUL* THAN A *LOCOMOTIVE*, RIGHT, TOM?

LOLA-- THE *LAST* THING WE NEED IS *TROUBLE* WITH THE F.C.C. ...

SOFTENING *UP*-- SHE'LL START *TALKING* SOON--

--WHAT'S THAT *SOUND*--

--THE FLOOR--

--IT'S *SHAKING*--

--NOT AN EARTHQUAKE. DO *NOT* PANIC. WHATEVER IT IS, IT'S *LOCALIZED*-- AND MOVING ACROSS GOTHAM'S *SOUTH* SIDE...

NEWS4

BBBBBLLLLLLLLLLLLLLLFMPP

NO--
NO--

POOM

--NOT
HIM--

--NOT
NOW--

HAH!

THE ROOM GOES
HOT--METAL
EXPLODES--

BRAPP

SPKAM SPKAM SPKAM SPKAM SPKAM

--I
HAVE
YOU--

SSSSSSSSSSSSKREFEEE

BRUCE--
WE HAVE
TO TALK.

I'M BUSY TONIGHT.
YOU'VE JUST COST
ME HOURS.

TOMORROW MORNING,
MY PLACE. STAY OUT
OF MY WAY UNTIL
THEN.

SOMETHING *HURLS* ITSELF INTO THE *SKY*.

SOMETHING *LEAPS* A TALL *BUILDING* WITH A *SINGLE BOUND*.

...SOVIET REPRESENTATIVES STORMED OUT OF THE HALL. REPEATING THIS LATE-BREAKING STORY--U.S./SOVIET TALKS ON THE CORTO MALTESE CRISIS HAVE BROKEN *DOWN*.

TERMING U.S. MILITARY SUPPORT OF THE REGIME OF GENERAL MONTALBAN AS "FASCIST AGGRESSION," THE SOVIETS PLEDGED A "TOTAL MILITARY COMMITMENT." THIS HAS BEEN A NEWS SIX *SPECIAL REPORT*.

...BODIES OF A *PUSHER* AND JUNKIE FOUND *HACKED* TO *PIECES* IN A WEST END TENEMENT. MEMBERS OF THE DISBANDED *MUTANT* GANG ARE CARRYING OUT THEIR THREAT TO GOTHAM'S UNDERWORLD.

THE MUTANTS ARE *DEAD*. THE MUTANTS ARE *HISTORY*. THIS IS THE MARK OF THE *FUTURE*. *GOTHAM CITY* BELONGS TO THE *BATMAN*.

NEWS 6 SPECIAL REPORT

NEWS 6 SPECIAL REPORT

ISSUES WITHIN ISSUES

DO NOT *EXPECT* ANY FURTHER *STATEMENTS*. THE *SONS* OF THE *BATMAN* DO NOT *TALK*. WE *ACT*. LET GOTHAM'S CRIMINALS *BEWARE*. THEY ARE ABOUT TO ENTER *HELL*.

BATMAN'S *CULPABILITY* FOR THIS ATROCITY IS OUR SUBJECT TONIGHT. WITH US IS THE WORLD'S LEADING EXPERT ON THE SOCIOLOGICAL IMPACT OF THE BATMAN-- DR. BARTHOLOMEW *WOLPER*.

BATMAN IS A MENACE TO SOCIETY.

NOW, I KNOW THAT'S SOMETHING OF AN *OUTDATED* TERM. SURE SOUNDS *STRANGE*, COMING OUT OF MY *MOUTH*. NONETHELESS, IT *APPLIES*. DESPITE MY *ALERTING* THE CITY TO THE *INEVITABLE CONSEQUENCES*--

--*NOTHING* HAS BEEN DONE TO STOP THIS PSYCHOSOCIAL *INFECTION*. BATMAN SHOULD BE CONSIDERED *PERSONALLY* RESPONSIBLE FOR EVERY HUMAN BEING MURDERED BY THIS GANG.

MY ORDERS WERE *SPECIFIC*--

WATCH IT--

YEAH, BUT...

--STILL, YOU MADE YOURSELF *VISIBLE* TO BRUNO. I WILL NOT TOLERATE *INSUBORDINATION*--

--CAREFUL--

...BUT BACK *THERE*-- WAS THAT *HIM*?

...THE HALL IS *SILENT,* AS THE MAN WHO HAS BEEN *POLICE COMMISSIONER* OF GOTHAM CITY FOR *TWENTY-SIX YEARS* STEPS TO THE *PODIUM*...

NICE WATCH.

... JAMES GORDON DRAWS A FOND *CHUCKLE* FROM THE AUDIENCE...

LADIES AND GENTLEMEN... IT IS MY PLEASURE TO INTRODUCE YOU TO YOUR NEW *POLICE COMMISSIONER.* I DO NOT ENVY HER THE NEXT FEW YEARS. THE JOB HAS FEW REWARDS.

THE BEST YOU CAN *HOPE* FOR IS THAT WHEN YOU'RE *FINISHED* WITH IT, THINGS AREN'T AS LOUSY AS THEY WOULD'VE BEEN *WITHOUT* YOU. ELLEN YINDEL IS EMINENTLY QUALIFIED FOR THIS JOB...

TO ATTEMPT TO QUOTE HER *OUTSTANDING RECORD* IN THE MINUTES I'M ALLOWED WOULD BE A *DISSERVICE* TO HER. RATHER, I OFFER MY *SYMPATHY,* IN THE KNOWLEDGE OF WHAT SHE FACES.

IF YOU *DISOBEY,* EVER AGAIN--

--YOU'RE *FIRED.*

SHE FACES A CITY OF *THIEVES* AND *MURDERERS* AND *HONEST* PEOPLE TOO FRIGHTENED TO *HOPE.* SHE FACES LIFE-AND-DEATH *DECISIONS,* EVERY HOUR TO COME. SOME WILL *TORTURE* HER.

WE *GOING* SOMEWHERE OR WHAT?

TO THE ONLY SOLID LEAD I'VE GOT LEFT, ROBIN. A MAN NAMED *ABNER.*

I'LL SEND ROBIN HOME.

I'LL HELP THE EMERGENCY TEAMS AS BEST I CAN.

I'LL COUNT THE DEAD, ONE BY ONE.

I'LL ADD THEM TO THE LIST, JOKER.

THE LIST OF ALL THE PEOPLE I'VE MURDERED--

-- BY LETTING YOU LIVE.

JUST CAN'T SLEEP.

SHOULD SLEEP.

SHOULD BE FRESH TOMORROW.

TOMORROW I GO FREE.

FISTFUL OF ENTERTAINMENT TOMORROW NIGHT, WITH DR. RUTH WEISENHEIMER, THE WET HAMBURGER BUN CONTEST, AND A MAN WHO'S BROUGHT A LOT OF SMILES TO THE WORLD. GO TO BED.

-- BUT I JUST CAN'T SLEEP.

...TWELVE KILLED IN A MYSTERIOUS EXPLOSION THAT LEVELED A BAY RIDGE APARTMENT BUILDING ...THE RESCUE TEAM SIGHTED BATMAN AT THE SCENE...

...FOLLOWING HER ARREST ORDER FOR THE BATMAN, COMMISSIONER YINDEL FILED A FORMAL PROTEST WITH THE MEDIA COUNCIL AGAINST THE JOKER'S APPEARANCE ON THE DAVID ENDOCHRINE SHOW...

THE COUNCIL DENIED HER PROTEST... THE BODY OF THREE-TIME LOSER HECTOR MENDEZ WAS FOUND IN AN EAST SIDE ALLEY. HE HAD BEEN LITERALLY SKINNED ALIVE...

...THE AMERICAN HOSTAGES GUILD HAS DECLARED A GENERAL STRIKE, IN RESPONSE TO TREATMENT OF THEIR MEMBERS IN THE RECENT LIBYAN INCIDENT...

GOOD MORNING, GOTHAM!

GOOD MORNING, GOTHAM!

GOOD MORNING, GOTHAM!

GOOD MORNING, GOTHAM!

WHAT CAN I SAY ABOUT OUR NEXT GUEST THAT HASN'T BEEN SAID BEFORE? PAUL?

HE'S A *KOOK*, DAVE. A *MANIAC*. A REAL *LUNATIC*. NO, I MEAN IT. HE'S A *NUT*.

SO MANY *FACES*--SO *DIFFERENT* FROM ONE ANOTHER...

...SO *FEW* SMILES...

THOKK

KLUDD

OVER THERE--

I SEE HIM--

JESUS, HE'S--

SMOKE'S CLEARING!

WE GOT HIM--

TK TK TK TK TK TK TK

WE MUST NOT
REMIND
THEM THAT
GIANTS
WALK THE
EARTH.

...URGING THE PUBLIC NOT TO WORRY, THE PRESIDENT HAS PLACED STRATEGIC AIR COMMANDS ON *RED ALERT.* "WE WON'T MAKE THE *FIRST MOVE*," SAID THE PRESIDENT, "BUT WE'RE READY TO MAKE THE *LAST.*"

THE *POPE* TODAY DECLARED THAT THE CHURCH'S STAND ON *CONTRACEPTION* WILL NOT CHANGE, DESPITE YESTERDAY'S *FIREBOMBING* OF ST. PETER'S SQUARE... AND, IN *LOCAL* NEWS...

MY HEAD GOES *LIGHT* AND THE *SMOKE* COATS THE INSIDE OF MY *MOUTH* AND LEAVES A PATCH OF RED-HOT GRAVEL AT THE BASE OF MY *THROAT.*

I STOPPED DOING THIS TO MYSELF FIVE YEARS AGO...

COMMISSIONER -WHITTAKER'S GONE ALL *SICK.*

HE'S JUST A *ROOKIE...*

SEND HIM HOME, MERKEL. TELL HIM IT'S ALL RIGHT.

...*TWO HUNDRED AND SIX* WERE SLAIN DURING THE *JOKER'S* ESCAPE FROM THE *DAVID ENDOCHRINE SHOW* INCLUDING HOST ENDOCHRINE AND DR. BARTHOLOMEW WOLPER.

THE *JOKER* REPORTEDLY USED HIS DEADLY *SMILE* GAS ON THE CROWD. *COMMISSIONER YINDEL* REFUSED TO COMMENT ON THIS, OR ON THE ESCAPE OF THE *BATMAN,* WHICH LEFT TWELVE POLICE OFFICERS HOSPITALIZED...

KYLE
ESCORT SERVICE, INC.

YOU SHOULDN'T HAVE COME *BACK,* BRUCE.

AMERICAN EXPRESS CARDS WELCOME

THEY'VE *CHANGED.* YOU DON'T *KNOW* HOW THEY'VE CHANGED.

THEY'LL *KILL* YOU...

SELINA--

OH, JESUS.

I NEED YOUR *HELP.*

IT'S VERY IMPORTANT.

KLIK CHAK

YOU GET THE HELL OUT OF HERE

THE YEARS HAVE NOT BEEN KIND, SELINA...

MMFF

AH, SELINA--YOU SHOULD BE *GRATEFUL* I CHANGED MY *LIPSTICK.* YOU *ARE* GRATEFUL *?*...

YES... GRATEFUL...

NOW...YOUR GIRL *ELSIE* IS ESCORTING A *CONGRESSMAN* TONIGHT. MEETING HIM AT HIS *HOTEL.*

WHY DON'T YOU CALL ELSIE IN HERE?

COLD WAVES LAP GOTHAM HARBOR...

...LIKE THEY HAVE ALL THE TIME IN THE WORLD...

...SHE DOESN'T MAKE A SOUND...

GOOD SOLDIER. GOOD SOLDIER.

CEASE FIRE. IS THAT A KID WITH HIM?

BOY WONDER-- GOT TO BE.

CALL INGERSOLL, MERKEL. TELL HIM TO ADD CHILD ENDANGERMENT TO THE--

:SKRIKK: COMMISSIONER -- THIS IS BATMAN.

THE GOVERNOR'S LIFE IS IN DANGER. I HAVEN'T TIME TO SAVE HIM. IT'S UP TO YOU.

BY THEN THE P8I WAS IN IT AND THINGS WERE GETTING OUT OF HAND.

AND THERE WAS THAT TROUBLE WITH OLIVER.

WE ALMOST THREW A PARTY WHEN YOU RETIRED.

DO YOU REMEMBER WHY YOU RETIRED, BRUCE?

NO--JUST LOOK AT YOU--

--YOU'D DO IT AGAIN-- AND LIKE A MURDERER, YOU'D COVER IT UP AGAIN.

NOTHING MATTERS TO YOU--EXCEPT YOUR HOLY WAR.

THEY WERE CONSIDERING THEIR OPTIONS AND YOU WERE PROBABLY STILL LAUGHING WHEN WE CAME TO TERMS.

I GAVE THEM MY OBEDIENCE AND MY INVISIBILITY.

THEY GAVE ME A LICENSE AND LET US LIVE.

NO, I DON'T LIKE IT. BUT I GET TO SAVE LIVES --AND THE MEDIA STAYS QUIET.

BUT NOW THE STORM IS GROWING AGAIN--

--THEY'LL HUNT US DOWN AGAIN--

--BECAUSE OF YOU.

...COMMUNICATIONS BLACKOUT CONTINUES AT *CORTO MALTESE*, AS DO THE BIZARRE *NATURAL DISTURBANCES.* HUNDRED-MILE-AN-HOUR *WINDS* LASH THE PORT OF *SAN CONCEPCION*, SIXTY MILES *SOUTH* OF CORTO...

THEY COULD PUT ME IN A *HELICOPTER* AND FLY ME UP INTO THE AIR AND LINE THE BODIES HEAD TO TOE ON THE GROUND IN DELIGHTFUL GEOMETRIC PATTERNS LIKE AN ENDLESS JUNE TAYLOR DANCERS ROUTINE --

-- AND IT WOULD NEVER BE ENOUGH.

NO, I DON'T KEEP COUNT. BUT YOU DO.

AND I LOVE YOU FOR IT.

...PENTAGON CHIEF GENERAL *LUCIUS LOCKHEED* CONFIRMS THAT STRATEGIC AIR COMMAND STANDS AT *DEF CON THREE* -- A HEARTBEAT FROM DEPLOYMENT. "WE'RE PRIMED", SAYS LOCKHEED...

...APPREHENDED WHILE TRYING TO POISON THE GOTHAM RESERVOIR WERE FORMER MEMBERS OF THE *MUTANT GANG.* THEIR SKIN WAS PAINTED CHALK WHITE, THEIR HAIR DYED GREEN...

SOMEWHERE A *WOMAN CALLS OUT* FOR HER SON...

SOMEWHERE A *CALLIOPE* PLAYS THE SAME TUNE, AGAIN AND AGAIN...

...A TINY HAND TIGHTENS IT'S GRIP ON MY ARM...

...A GIRL OF THIRTEEN BREATHES IN SHARPLY, SUDDENLY, HER INNOCENCE LOST...

...IT ENDS TONIGHT, JOKER.

LANA, YOU *ASTONISH* ME. FIFTEEN POLICEMEN HOSPITALIZED -- HUNDREDS *DEAD* -- AND STILL YOU CLING TO THIS *HERO WORSHIP.* THOUGH HOW ANYONE CAN THINK OF A *DEFACTO MURDERER* AS A HERO...

BATMAN HASN'T KILLED ANYBODY, MORRIE.

NO, JOKER.

YOU'RE PLAYING THE WRONG GAME. THE OLD GAME.

TONIGHT YOU'RE TAKING NO HOSTAGES.

THUNK THUNK THUNK BLAM THUNK THUN AAAGGG

TONIGHT I'M TAKING NO PRISONERS.

BLAMM

OUT OF YOUR MIND--

CHECK THE STATISTICS, LANA DEAR--HECK, IF YOU TOSS IN THE VICTIMS OF HIS FAN CLUB, THE BATMAN-RELATED BODY COUNT IS UP THERE WITH A MINOR WAR.

IT IS A WAR, MORRIE--THOUGH HE SEEMS TO BE THE ONLY ONE WITH BALLS ENOUGH TO FIGHT IT.

WHO GAVE THIS THUG THE RIGHT TO DECLARE MARTIAL LAW, HM? LAST I HEARD, THAT TAKES AN ACT OF CONGRESS.

BILLY

GONE BILLY

CAN'T

BELIEVE I'M DOING THIS--

OH, REAL COO--

--LIKE ALL FAN--

BLAM

KPWEE

--BEFORE THE DOLL--

--WON'T DUST ME--

--LIKE GOODYEAR THERE--

KLIK KLAK

KLIK KLAK

KLIKKLAK

TK TK TK

--DOES THE MAXIMUM FLASH--

KLIK KLAK

BLAM

KLIK KLAK

--OUT OF *BULLETS* -- GOT A *SHOT* -- ACE THE *BOMB* -- EASY SHOT--

--*REAL GOOD, CARRIE* -- *LUNCHROOM* OR *WHAT* -- LIKE YOU'VE *GOT* ALL NIGHT--

--SOME *ROBIN* -- REAL COOL -- JUST *ACE* IT -- *EASY* SHOT--

--*EASY*--

EXCUSE ME.

I'M TOO LATE ...FOR THE ONE ON THE BOARDWALK...

IT HAPPENS... SO SLOWLY...

...IT HAPPENS ...IN FIVE SECONDS...

...THE BLADE IS SHARP...

...I BARELY FELT IT ENTER MY STOMACH...

...HE'S TALKING... I CAN'T HEAR HIM...

...SOMETHING IS ROARING... I CAN'T... HEAR ANYTHING...

...HIS NECK... ...WILL HAVE TO DO...

SHKK

...HE'S MOVING ...MORE QUICKLY THAN I AM...

...STABBING...

THNK

SHKK

THNK

SHKK KRAK KK

...THE ROAR... IS FADING... I HEAR... VOICES...

--SHEER *PANDEMONIUM* HERE AT THE *COUNTY FAIR*, LOLA! THE JOKER HAS BEEN SIGHTED--*SIXTEEN CUB SCOUTS* HAVE BEEN FOUND *DEAD*--*DOZENS* HAVE BEEN *WOUNDED* BY *EXPLOSIONS*--

--AND *BATMAN* HAS BEEN SEEN--HE AND THE JOKER EXCHANGED GUNFIRE IN A CROWD-- HEY--WHAT--LOLA-- THEY'RE EVACUATING THE *COUNTY FAIR*--

...VOICES CALLING ME... A KILLER...

...I WISH I WERE...

THEY'RE GONE...?

...THE WITNESSES, I MEAN...

I'M REALLY...VERY DISAPPOINTED WITH YOU, MY SWEET... THE MOMENT WAS... PERFECT... ...AND YOU... DIDN'T HAVE THE *NERVE*...

PARALYSIS... REALLY...

THE DARK KNIGHT FALLS

CHRIST IT'S--

SPREADING --IT'S--

FIRE'S SPREADING--

HOLY--

POOM

POOM POOM

ROBIN...

...COME IN... ROBIN...

KLIK KLAK

SUMMON... THE COPTER...

FOLLOW... MY SIGNAL...

...YES, SIR. I'M PUNCHING THE CODE IN--

UH-OH-- GOT TROUBLE, BOSS.

WHUP WHUP

KLIK KLAK

ATTENTION. AS IN MEDIA.

WHUP WHUP

KLIK KLAK

KLIK KLAK

CLOSER-- MOVE IN CLOSER-- LOLA-- CAN YOU SEE IT?-- LIVE FROM THE NEWS TWO COPTER-- IT'S ROBIN-- THE BOY WONDER!

HE'S YOUNG-- CAN'T BE OLDER THAN THIRTEEN-- HE'S RIDING THE ROLLER COASTER-- HE'S WAIT-- HE'S--

KLIK KLAK

MFF

FREEZE, YOU--

ONE OF THEM HAS THE *BRAINS* TO JUMP *CLEAR...*

--YOU SON OF A BITCH... *FREEZE--*

CUTE *GUN...*

WHDD

CHK CHAK

STOP...

...STOP

LAUGHING...

WE'RE MOVING *IN*, MEN-- NO TIME TO *WASTE--*

IF IT'S NOT A *COP--* SHOOT IT.

BLOW THAT BASTARD'S *HEAD OFF--*

--SWEAR I'LL BLOW HIS GOD DAMN *HEAD OFF--*

SWAT TEAM...

THEY'RE *ARMORED...* WON'T HAVE TO...*RESTRAIN* MYSELF...

JUST ENOUGH TIME TO--

BLACKED *OUT...* CAN'T AFFORD THAT...

GOOD... DIDN'T GET THE *GUN* WET...

I'LL *NEED* IT... PROVIDED I CAN FIT MY *FINGER* IN THE *TRIGGER GUARD...*

SOMETHING ...TO KEEP AN OLD MAN AWAKE...

...AND SOMETHING *ELSE...*

...TO BRING THE *HOUSE* DOWN...

PROPERTY DAMAGE.

AUTO.

PFAM

POOM

I KNEW SHE'D MAKE IT...

...I MIGHT'VE... AT HER AGE...

HNNGG-G

KCHOW KCHOWN

WHUP WHUP WHUP

BRAKA BRAKK

YINDEL'S GOING TO *KILL* US...

GOTHAM CITY WILL NO LONGER *TOLERATE* THIS FLAGRANT VIOLATION OF THE LAW-- THIS VIOLENT *ASSAULT* ON THE VERY UNDERPINNINGS OF OUR SOCIETY...

BY ATTACKING GOTHAM'S POLICE, BATMAN HAS REVEALED HIMSELF AS AN UNQUALIFIED *MENACE.* I HAVE INSTRUCTED THE ATTORNEY GENERAL TO PLACE THE STATE POLICE AT GOTHAM'S DISPOSAL...

...THE JOKER'S BODY FOUND *MUTILATED* AND *BURNED*... *MURDER* IS ADDED TO THE CHARGES AGAINST THE *BATMAN*...

BRUCE. IT'S OVER.

YOU LOOK TIRED, KENT.

WELL, YOU'VE *EARNED* A GOOD NIGHT'S *SLEEP.*

HECK OF A POLICE ACTION, IF YOU ASK ME...

I DIDN'T...

YOU CAN *SAY* WHAT YOU *WANT.* YOU CAN *CALL* HIM WHAT YOU *WANT.* YOU DON'T HAVE TO WALK DOWN AVENUE D AT NIGHT.

YOU DON'T HAVE TO HEAR THE *SUCKING* SOUNDS THEY MAKE EVERY TIME YOU WALK BY. *THIS* ONE. HE'D BEEN WORKING THE NERVE UP FOR *WEEKS* BEFORE HE WAS *HORNY* ENOUGH...

...NO, HORNY HE *WASN'T.* HE WAS JUST LOOKING TO *HURT* SOMEBODY AND HE'S THE KIND WHO HURTS *WOMEN.* I WISH THEY WERE *RARE.* HE GAVE HIMSELF AN EXCUSE...

SO NOW HE'S *GIGGLING* LIKE HE'S *TURNED ON!* I FIGURE HE'S *SERIOUS* ENOUGH TO RUN *AFTER* ME. I GO FOR THE *MACE.*

THE CREEP'S PULLING OUT HIS WEAPON WHEN THERE'S THIS SHRIEK.

STRAIGHT OUT OF *HELL* THERE'S THIS SHRIEK...

...IT TURNS INTO A *GROWL*-- FLAPPING OF WINGS--*BIG* WINGS--

-- SOMETHING *WET* HAPPENS TO THE CREEP--

--A SIDE OF *BEEF* SLAMS INTO THE *LAMPPOST*--

--A *SWITCHBLADE* SNAPS OPEN--

BONES START *POPPING* INSIDE THE *CREEP*-- HE'S *SCREAMING* AND *BEGGING*--

--WHAT *GRABBED* HIM IS *LAUGHING* AND SO AM *I*...

AND THE MAN WHO *ASSAULTED* YOU?

STILL IN THE HOSPITAL.

HE'S *OLD*, HE'S *ALMOST DEAD*...

SUTURE.

HE'S *GOING* TO BE *OKAY*, RIGHT?

HE'LL *LIVE*...

DO NOT EXPECT ANY *FURTHER* STATEMENTS. THE *SONS* OF THE *BATMAN* DO *NOT* TALK. WE *ACT*. LET GOTHAM'S CRIMINALS *BEWARE*. THEY ARE ABOUT TO ENTER *HELL*.

THE MUTANTS ARE *DEAD*. THE MUTANTS ARE *HISTORY*. THIS IS THE *MARK* OF THE *FUTURE*. *GOTHAM CITY* BELONGS TO THE *BATMAN*.

...THE *SONS* OF THE *BATMAN* HAVE STRUCK AGAIN. *JEFF STRICKEN* WAS CLOSING UP THE *SOUTH STREET 7-11* WHEN HE BECAME BOTH *WITNESS*-- AND *VICTIM*...

THEY'RE *YOUNGER* THAN YOU'D THINK--*THIS* ONE WAS, ANYWAY. COULDN'T HAVE BEEN OLDER THAN *SIXTEEN*...THAT'S RIGHT, THERE WAS JUST *ONE* OF THEM...

...BUT I'M GETTING AHEAD OF MYSELF. IT ALL *STARTED* WHEN THREE NIXONS CAME INTO THE STORE. WHAT?... NO, I DID *NOT* GO FOR THE ALARM. THEY DON'T *PAY* ME ENOUGH FOR *SUICIDE.*

I WAS CLEARING OUT THE REGISTER WHEN THAT OFF-DUTY COP CAME UP FROM THE BACK.

HE ONLY SAW *TWO* OF THE NIXONS.

THE COP WAS STILL *TWITCHING* WHEN THEY HEADED FOR THE DOOR.

I HEARD A *THUNDERCLAP.*

I'D HAVE *LOVED* TO HAVE *WARNED* HIM.

THE *TALL* NIXON WENT FOR HIS PIECE.

MORE THUNDER.

THE *LAST* ONE WATCHED THE *S.O.B.* RELOAD HIS *SHOTGUN* AND DIDN'T SAY A *WORD.*

THEN THE *S.O.B.*, HE TOLD ME I SHOULD'VE PUT UP A *FIGHT* WITH THE NIXONS. SAID I DIDN'T *DESERVE* TO RUN A *CASH REGISTER.* HE GRABBED A PAIR OF *WIRE CUTTERS* --

THE NIXONS ARE THE NEWEST SPLINTER GROUP OF THE *MUTANT ARMY,* WHICH EXPERTS BELIEVE *DISBANDED* WHEN THE *BATMAN* DEFEATED THEIR LEADER. TOM?

TWENTY
MILLION
DIE BY
FIRE...

...IF I
AM WEAK...

I COULD BE SITTING AT HOME CATCHING UP ON MY READING-- YES, SOME OF US STILL READ-- IF NOT FOR SARAH AND THE ONE MORE THING SHE ALWAYS NEEDS FROM THE GROCERY STORE.

THIS TIME IT'S BEANS. VEGETARIAN BEANS. TOOK ME TEN MINUTES TO FIGURE OUT THAT IT ISN'T IN THE HEALTH FOOD SECTION. IT'S JUST BEANS WITHOUT MEAT.

TEN MINUTES OF MY LIFE.

I NEED A CIGAR.

TWENTY-THREE DAYS WITHOUT. EVERYBODY'S PROUD AS HELL.

ONE CIGAR AND EVERYTHING WOULD BE RIGHT WITH THE WORLD...

WHAT--

WHAT'S SHE SAYING--

OH, GOD, NO...

QUIET-- I CAN'T HEAR--

A *SOVIET NUCLEAR WARHEAD*-- SECONDS FROM *DETONATION* OVER *CORTO MALTESE*--

THIS IS *IT*, FOLKS--*FIRST STRIKE!* TOM?

LOLA CHONG GIVES GOOD NEWS

NEWS 2 GOTHO

CAREFUL--BE *CAREFUL* HOW YOU *PUT* THINGS, LOLA. THIS IS *ONE* MISSILE-- THERE ARE NO INDICATIONS THAT THIS IS PART OF A *FULL-SCALE ATTACK*...

TELL THAT TO THE AMERICAN TROOPS *STATIONED* THERE, TOM.

HOLD IT... WE'VE JUST GOTTEN WORD THAT IT'S *NOT* A CONVENTIONAL NUCLEAR WARHEAD--WE SWITCH YOU NOW TO *DAN MUSK*, ABOARD THE *NEWS TWO SHUTTLE*. WHAT'S THE WORD, DAN?

STILL *COLLATING*, LOLA-- BUT IT'S A *BIG* ONE-- *HEAVY MEGATONNAGE*-- WITH *UNUSUAL COMPUTER ACTIVITY*-- WE CAN'T BE *CERTAIN* OF ITS CAPABIL- ITIES...

...AT THE VERY LEAST, *CORTO* WILL BE *LEVELED*-- THE *FIRES* MIGHT SPREAD TO MAINLAND *SOUTH AMERICA*-- SHOULD IT GENERATE A SUFFICIENT *MAGNETIC PULSE*, THERE MIGHT--

THANKS FOR THE *DATA*, DAN, BUT WE'LL ALL KNOW SOON *ENOUGH* WHAT IT CAN DO. RIGHT NOW, WE'VE GOT AUTHOR *HARLAN ELLISON* IN THE STUDIO...

MR. *PRESIDENT* --GIVE THE *WORD*--

NOW YOU JUST KEEP YOUR SHIRT ON, LUCIUS...

MR. *PRESIDENT* --WE'LL LOOK LIKE *WIMPS* IF WE DON'T--

--LET'S SEE WHAT OUR OWN LITTLE DETERRENT CAN DO...

MAYBE DURING A BREAK BETWEEN POLICE ACTIONS, ONE OF YOUR MILITARY FRIENDS TOLD YOU WHAT AN ELECTROMAGNETIC PULSE IS. AND MAYBE YOU LISTENED, CLARK.

ALL YOU NEED TO GENERATE THE PULSE IS THE ORGANIZED DETONATION OF A FEW DOZEN NUCLEAR WARHEADS.

THAT, OR A SPECIAL KIND OF NUKE THAT BOTH SIDES HAVE BEEN TRYING TO DEVELOP...

Sweetheart, the last of the readings gave a hint of what would happen.

When the computer failed, I knew for sure.

failed, I knew for sure. There's no point in explaining it to the crew. We're all dead anyway—as dead as this shuttle.

You'll never get to read thi

You'll never get to read this letter. It'll burn up with me when our orbit deteriorates. Still, my last thoughts will be a prayer for you, for humanity...

...and for planet Earth.

Nothing could stop the Russians from emptying their silos at us now. We'd have no defense, no way to retaliate.

The one hope we have is that the decision to murder billions has to be made by a human being.

...YES, CLARK. BOTH SIDES.

THE AMERICAN NAME FOR IT IS COLDBRINGER. IT'S DESIGNED TO CAUSE MAXIMUM DAMAGE TO THE ENVIRONMENT-- ALL THE WHILE SPARING THE INDUSTRIAL SITES YOUR FRIENDS REGARD SO HIGHLY.

SINCE MY OWN ATOMS AREN'T BOUNCING AROUND THE STRATOSPHERE--

--SINCE GOTHAM CITY SQUATS LIKE A GREAT BLACK GRAVEYARD--

--SINCE WAYNE MANOR'S EMERGENCY GENERATOR HASN'T KICKED IN-- AND ROBIN'S WATCH HAS STOPPED--

--I'LL ASSUME RUSSIA HAS TAKEN THE LEAD IN THE ARMS RACE.

I KEEP TRACK OF THESE THINGS, CLARK.

ONE OF US HAS TO.

THE DUMP.

IT'S A BREEDING GROUND FOR INSECTS AND RODENTS.

SOME RODENTS FLY.

JUST HIS VOICE.

JUST HIM.

EEEKKRKKK

ALL RUNNING AWAY--LOOKS BAD-- --I'M CRYING BUT IT'S JUST THE SMOKE--

--SMOKE-- DOESN'T IT FIGURE--

KK

DOWN THERE--

COPS--

AIN'T FAN--

DON'T SHIV--

SOMETHING EXPLODES--

--RIGHT ON MY BLOCK--

--A GAS MAIN--

BUDDA

...BULLFROGS, WHO SLEPT FOR YEARS IN DRIED-OUT RIVERBEDS... THEN DUG THEIR WAY TO THE SURFACE WHEN THE RAINS CAME...

NOW... THERE IS ONLY BLACKENED GLASS...

...ENDLESS FLAME...

OUR PEOPLE, BRUCE. YOU LAUGH AT THEM.

THEY CAN DO THIS... AND YOU LAUGH...

...THEY CAN SPLIT THE VERY FABRIC OF REALITY... BLAST A HUNDRED THOUSAND TONS OF SAND INTO THE SKY...

...BLOTTING OUT THE SOURCE OF ALL MY POWER... THE HOPE FOR SCREAMING MILLIONS...

MAGNETIC STORM ...YOU HAVE EVERY REASON TO BE OUTRAGED, MOTHER EARTH... YOU HAVE GIVEN THEM... EVERYTHING...

THEY ARE TINY AND STUPID AND VICIOUS ...BUT PLEASE... LISTEN TO THEM...

PLEASE...I AM SLOW AND DYING...

I NEED ONLY... REACH THE SUN...

YOU ARE...SO GENEROUS...

YOU GIVE ME... YOUR BEAUTIFUL JUNGLE...

I SWEAR...

...YOUR ADOPTED SON WILL HONOR YOU.

FROM MY BUILDING--

--SHE SCREAMS--

SARAH'S HEIGHT--

--SARAH'S HAIR--

A SKIRT--

--THAT COULD BE SARAH'S--

TRY NOT TO JUDGE THEM TOO *HARSHLY.* IT WAS A *CRUEL* TEST, FOR ALL OF US...

...AND, WE CAN HOPE, A *LESSON*...

NONE OF US CAN LOOK BACK ON THAT NIGHT WITHOUT *SHAME.* EVEN *BEFORE* IT ALL... I WAS *WRAPPED* IN MYSELF. YOU SEE, I HAVE ALWAYS BEEN RATHER *SENSITIVE* TO *NOISE*...

...AND THAT *BOY*-- HE SEEMED TO KEEP PACE WITH ME *DELIBERATELY,* TAKING THE JOY FROM MY *EVENING* WALK...

...WITH HIS HORRIBLY LOUD RADIO...

WHEN IT *SHRIEKED,* I *BLAMED* THE BOY. TRUTH TO TELL, I TURNED TO *CONFRONT* HIM...

...THEN I NOTICED HIS *OWN* CONFUSION -- AND THE *DARKNESS* THAT SEEMED TO FALL ACROSS THE ENTIRE *CITY.* I HEARD *SHOUTS*...

YES, I WAS *SHOUTING.* WHAT DO YOU *EXPECT* ? I HAPPENED TO BE UP AGAINST A *BITCH* OF A *DEADLINE.* WHAT ?... ...YES, OF *COURSE* I'D HEARD ABOUT THE *BOMB.* BUT I'VE GOT PROBLEMS OF MY OWN.

I'M NOT CRAZY ABOUT GETTING OUT OF MY CAR-- NOT IN *THAT* NEIGHBORHOOD--

--BUT I KNOW I BETTER CALL THE *AGENCY* AND MAKE SURE MY *ASS* IS COVERED.

SO I'M BARELY STANDING *UP* WHEN THERE'S *THIS EXPLOSION* KNOCKS ME *FLAT*--

MY ANKLE FEELS LIKE IT'S *BROKEN*-- SOMEBODY IS GOING TO GET *SUED*--

...THEN HE STRAIGHTENS UP AND GRINS AT ME LIKE IT'S FUNNY.

HE CAN'T DIE...

TURNS OUT SARAH HAD GONE TO THE GROCERY STORE.

TURNS OUT SARAH FORGOT TO TELL ME SHE NEEDED MILK.

ONE MORE THING.

AFTER THE MOB LEFT, THE EXPLOSIONS CONTINUED. THE FIRES WERE EVERY-WHERE...

...I WAS BARELY CONSCIOUS...IF NOT FOR THE BOY, I...

THAT'S RIGHT. THE BOY WITH THE RADIO. HE PULLED ME CLEAR. SAVED MY LIFE. WHEN BATMAN DROPPED OFF THE MEDICAL SUPPLIES, THE BOY PASSED THEM AROUND...

...HE WAS AT MY SIDE TILL MORNING, HELPING THE BURNED.

BUT, OF COURSE, THERE WASN'T ANY MORNING ...

...ONE WEEK LATER, IT'S STILL DARK AT HIGH NOON IN GOTHAM CITY. IT'S STILL WINTER IN AUGUST. HERE'S CARLA SHRIEK TO EXPLAIN...

LOLA, THE SOVIET *COLDBRINGER* WAS DESIGNED TO *INDUCE* THE *ENVIRONMENTAL EFFECTS* OF *FULL-SCALE NUCLEAR WAR.* FIRST, IT GENERATED THE *PULSE* THAT BLACKED OUT--

ON THAT *PULSE*-- DON'T MISS OUR *SPECIAL* TONIGHT-- YOUR FAVORITE *STARS* ARE ASKED "*WHERE WERE YOU WHEN THE LIGHTS WENT OUT?*" CARLA?

LOLA, THE *PULSE* WAS ONLY THE *BEGINNING.* WEATHER PATTERNS ACROSS THE HEMISPHERE HAVE BEEN *COMPLETELY* DISRUPTED--

THEY SURE HAVE, *CARLA,* AND SO HAS MY *WARDROBE.* THIS IS THE *COLDEST* DAY OF THE *YEAR.* I DON'T KNOW *WHAT* TO WEAR THESE DAYS...

STARVING

RIOTS

CIVIL AR IN E MID-EST

CUBANS WON'T BUDGE

MEDIA PUSH

CREDIBILITY DISASTER

...NO, MR. PRESIDENT. I'M AFRAID HE'LL *NEVER* LET ME BRING HIM IN *ALIVE*...

THE *COLDEST,* LOLA-- UNTIL *TOMORROW.* THE BOMB'S *BLAST* THRUST HUNDREDS OF *MILLIONS* OF *TONS* OF *SOOT* INTO THE *STRATOSPHERE*--

--CREATING A *BLACK CLOUD* THAT COVERS THE *AMERICAS,* BLOTTING OUT THE *SUN*-- DEPRIVING US OF *LIGHT* AND *HEAT*...

...*PEOPLE* ARE *FREEZING* TO DEATH BY THE *THOUSANDS*...THE DAMAGE TO *CROPS* COULD WELL BRING ON A *FAMINE*...

I'M SURPRISED HE TOOK THE CHANCE OF COMING TO *AMERICA*-- WITH *CLARK* IN THE COUNTRY--

--BUT *OLIVER* HAS ALWAYS LIVED BY HIS *IMPULSES.*

THIS *PARTICULAR IMPULSE* I CAN *UNDERSTAND*...

YOU'VE ALWAYS HAD IT *WRONG,* BRUCE...

...GIVING THEM SUCH A BIG *TARGET.* SURE, YOU PLAY IT *MYSTERIOUS*-- BUT IT'S A *LOUD* KIND OF *MYSTERIOUS,* MAN. ESPECIALLY *LATELY.*

YOU GOT TO LEARN HOW TO MAKE THOSE SONS OF BITCHES WORK FOR YOU. LOOK-- IT'S BEEN *FIVE YEARS* SINCE I BLEW OUT OF *PRISON*--

--AND YOU *KNOW* I'VE KEPT *BUSY*--

...*COMPUTER FAILURE* WAS RESPONSIBLE FOR THE *SINKING* OF THE U.S. NUCLEAR SUBMARINE *VALIANT,* PENTAGON SOURCES DISCLOSED TODAY...NO HANDS WERE *LOST*...

--AND THEY'VE BEEN *COVERING* FOR ME, JUST LIKE THEY COVERED UP MY *ESCAPE*. SURE, THEY'D *LOVE* TO FROST ME...

...LONG AS THEY CAN *DO* IT WITHOUT ADMITTING I *EXIST*.

SNAKT

BUT *YOU*, BRUCE--

--MAN, THEY *HAVE* TO KILL YOU.

OLIVER-- WHAT DO YOU *WANT*?

I ALWAYS *KNEW* IT'D GET DOWN TO *YOU* AND THE BIG BLUE *SCHOOLBOY*. PLANET'S TOO *BIG* FOR THE *TWO* OF YOU.

WHEN IT ALL COMES *DOWN*...

...I WANT A *PIECE* OF HIM. A *SMALL* PIECE WILL DO, FOR *OLD TIMES* SAKE, YOU KNOW...

...IT STILL *HURTS* WHEN IT'S *COLD*...

...NOTHING WE CAN'T HANDLE, FOLKS. WE'RE STILL *AMERICA*-- AND I'M STILL *PRESIDENT*.

WHO *WAS* THAT SPUD? TALKS LIKE MY *DAD*.

HE USED TO FIGHT *CRIME*.

...THE *PRESIDENT* HAS IMPOSED *LIMITED MARTIAL LAW*, THEREBY DEPLOYING *MILITARY* AID TO LAW-ENFORCEMENT AGENCIES AGAINST OUTBREAKS OF *VIOLENCE* AND *LOOTING*...

RIGHT *THERE*-- IN THAT *SADDLE*--IS ALL THE REASON I NEED...

...IT'S ALMOST *FRIGHTENING* HOW *QUICKLY* SHE'S LEARNING TO RIDE...

SHE HAS DECADES -- *DECADES*, LEFT TO HER...

...*NEW YORK, CHICAGO, METROPOLIS*-- EVERY CITY IN *AMERICA* IS CAUGHT IN THE GRIP OF A NATIONAL *PANIC*-- WITH ONE EXCEPTION. RIGHT, TOM?...

PANIC!

...*THEN*-- A BLAST OF *HEAT*--

--FROM THE *SKY*--

WHERE?

--AND IT *BEGINS*...

CRIME ALLEY.

...THAT'S *RIGHT*, LOLA. THANKS TO THE *BATMAN* AND HIS VIGILANTE GANG, *GOTHAM'S* STREETS ARE *SAFE*-- UNLESS YOU TRY TO COMMIT A *CRIME*...

...HEALING QUITE *POORLY*, MASTER BRUCE.

SHALL I PREPARE ANOTHER *STIMULANT?* WHY *DELAY* YOUR VERY FIRST *CARDIAC ARREST?*

OLIVER--MAYBE OLIVER WAS *RIGHT*... ALL ALONG...

...*CRAZY* AS IT SOUNDS...

...*BLOODY* WALKING *HOSPITAL BED*...

THAT'S *ENOUGH*, ALFRED.

...IN THE PAST WEEK , SEVENTY THREE *VIOLENT ATTACKS* ON WOULD-BE *LOOTERS* HAVE BEEN ATTRIBUTED BY WITNESSES TO THE *BATMAN* AND HIS *GANG*...

...WHEN YOU *CAME* FOR ME... IN THE CAVE... I WAS JUST *SIX* YEARS OLD...

...YOU WERE *ANCIENT*... *NOTHING* COULD KILL YOU...

...BUT THE *WAR*...

...IT DID NOT *BEGIN* THEN...

NO... IT WAS... TWO YEARS *LATER*... WHEN HER *NECKLACE* CAUGHT ON HIS *WRIST*...

...WHEN HE *SHOVED* HIS *PISTOL* TO HER *JAW* AND PULLED THE *TRIGGER*...

...AND EVERYTHING MY *MOTHER* WAS STRUCK THE PAVEMENT AS A BLOODY *WAD*...

THAT *NIGHT*... BEGAN THIRTY YEARS OF HUNTING *THIEVES* AND *MURDERERS*...

...IS *THAT* WHAT YOU *INTENDED?*...

...COMMISSIONER *YINDEL* REFUSED TO COMMENT ON THE CHARGE THAT GOTHAM'S *POLICE* HAVE BEEN *LAX* IN PURSUING THE *MURDER* CHARGE AGAINST THE *BATMAN*...

SOMEWHERE IN THE ENDLESS *NIGHT*... LIKE A *BELLOW* FROM A *WOUNDED BEAR*...

...THE *ANSWER* COMES...

...*ARMY TROOPS* HAVE EVACUATED THE *SLUM* KNOWN AS *CRIME ALLEY*--NO EXPLANATION IS GIVEN--*NEWS* COVERAGE HAS BEEN FLATLY *DENIED*--

THE *TIMING*...MUST BE *EXACT*...

...IN ONE *HOUR*... AT *MIDNIGHT*...

...A *GRAND DEATH*...

RUMORS FLY-- *ARMY HELICOPTERS* HOVER OVER THE *EMPTY* STREETS OF *CRIME ALLEY*--IS THIS A *MILITARY* EFFORT TO CAPTURE THE *BATMAN*--

THIS ONE YOU WON'T *BELIEVE*, CLARK.

MY BEST *TRICK*...

--OR IS THIS THE FINAL *BATTLE* BETWEEN TWO *TITANS* -- THE LAST STAND FOR THE CAPED CRUSADER--FACING THE *MIGHT* OF THE MAN OF STE-

SKRIKK

DO NOT ADJUST YOUR SET

...so frightfully FORMAL, his dark eyes FLASHING...

Alfred assured him that the villain had met justice.

...Master Bruce asked--no, DEMANDED... "the killer was CAUGHT. And PUNISHED."

KN

DETONATION T MINUS

00:11:24

00:11:23

He hits the ground on schedule.

One block from me.

Breathing a little FAST--

It's ROBIN'S TURN--

THE CHARGE COULD SINK A BATTLESHIP. I THINK HE FEELS IT.

POOM

WHUMP

SKREKK

ISN'T TONIGHT A SCHOOL NIGHT?

MORE WIND.

NOW HE'S TALKING-- TRYING TO REASON WITH ME. I CAN'T HEAR HIM, OF COURSE...

...NO, MY EARS ARE PROTECTED-- SO ALL I HAVE TO WORRY ABOUT IS MY TEETH--

--RATTLING FROM MY JAW--OR SHATTERING, LIKE EVERY WINDOW ON THE BLOCK--

--WHEN I HIT HIM WITH THE SONIC.

A NOSEBLEED --SO SOON, CLARK--

DON'T DROP NOW-- THE NIGHT IS YOUNG--

AND I HAVE--SO MUCH PLANNED--

--AND IT HAS TO END HERE-- ON THIS FILTHY PATCH OF STREET--

--WHERE MY PARENTS DIED...

...WHERE I CAN USE THE CITY'S POWER--

--EVERY WATT OF IT--

--TO FRY YOUR BRAIN--

--STILL TALKING-- KEEP TALKING, CLARK...

...YOU'VE ALWAYS KNOWN JUST WHAT TO SAY.

"YES"-- YOU ALWAYS SAY YES-- TO ANYONE WITH A BADGE-- OR A FLAG--

--NO GOOD--

-- THE FEEDBACK-- I'M NOT GETTING A HUNDREDTH OF WHAT YOU ARE--

--BUT IT'S GETTING BAD-- AHEAD OF SCHEDULE--

--WHAT DIDN'T HIT YOU-- AND ME-- FED THIS SUIT, CLARK--

--IT'S WAY PAST TIME YOU LEARNED WHAT IT MEANS--

--TO BE A MAN--

IT WASN'T *EASY* TO *SYNTHESIZE,* CLARK...

...TOOK *YEARS*...AND IT COST A *FORTUNE*...

...LUCKILY I HAD *BOTH*...

COME AND *GET* ME YOU *SONS OF--*

--WHA--

EYES DOWNSIDE, SPUD.

FIGURE WE GOT *ALL* WEEK...

HIYO GOD DAMN *SILVER.*

KOFF

BRUCE-- *YOUR HEART*--

YOU'RE BEGINNING TO GET THE *IDEA,* CLARK...

...THIS...IS THE *END*...

...FOR *BOTH* OF US...

-- TANK'S BREAKING *AWAY*--

--GOT THEM-- WHOLE *AREA'S* SURROUNDED--

--HEADING *ACROSS* THE PARKING LOT--

--WHAT--FELL *THROUGH*--

--WHAT THE *HELL*--

OH, *CHRIST*--

WATER MAIN-- WE *LOST* THEM--

--*CHRIST* WE *LOST* THEM--

WE COULD HAVE *CHANGED* THE *WORLD*...

...NOW... *LOOK* AT US...

I'VE BECOME... A *POLITICAL LIABILITY*... ...AND *YOU*...

...YOU'RE A *JOKE*...

The clock strikes TWELVE.

The ancient moor TREMBLES, beneath Alfred's feet.

Deep underground, COMPUTERS, holding every precious SECRET of the BATMAN, burst, and BURN...

Mrs. Wayne's priceless collection of PORCELAIN shatters, musically...

...the central mass of Wayne Manor SHUDDERS, as if ALIVE...

The world turns ruby RED. The manor roof RISES, madly, into the sky, riding a pillar of FLAME.

A jolt travels the length of Alfred's SPINE. Of course, he thinks, as his head goes light.

...empty STABLES fly apart like toothpick models...

...then VANISHES in a FLASH, bright as the sun.

How utterly proper.

DON'T TOUCH HIM--

...COMMEND HIS SOUL...

...CLOUD HAS ALMOST *COMPLETELY* CLEARED IN THE PAST SEVENTY-TWO HOURS. THE PRESIDENT HAS DECLARED A STATE OF *STABILIZED EMERGENCY*...

REPEATING THE WEEK'S TOP STORIES-- THE SPECTACULAR CAREER OF THE *BATMAN* CAME TO A TRAGIC CONCLUSION...

...AS THE CRIMEFIGHTER SUFFERED A *HEART ATTACK* WHILE BATTLING GOVERNMENT TROOPS.

HE HAS BEEN IDENTIFIED AS FIFTY-FIVE YEAR OLD BILLIONAIRE *BRUCE WAYNE*-- AND HIS *DEATH* HAS PROVEN AS MYSTERIOUS AS HIS *LIFE*...

SON OF A *BITCH*-- I *KNOW* WHO KILLED HIM--

SELINA-- THIS IS NO GOOD...

WAYNE MANOR WAS LEVELLED BY A SERIES OF EXPLOSIONS, SET APPARENTLY, BY WAYNE'S BUTLER, FOUND DEAD FROM A STROKE AT THE SCENE...

...FLAMES DESTROYED WHATEVER EVIDENCE MAY HAVE EXISTED AS TO BATMAN'S *METHODS*. ALSO MISSING, IT SEEMS, IS THE WAYNE *FORTUNE*...

...CAN'T BELIEVE HE HAD THE NERVE TO COME HERE...

INTERNAL REVENUE AGENTS INVESTIGATED WAYNE'S RECORDS, FINDING HIS EVERY *BANK ACCOUNT EMPTY*, EVERY *STOCK SOLD*...

...WHERE THE MONEY *WENT* IS ONE MORE SECRET WAYNE HAS TAKEN TO HIS GRAVE... HIS BODY WAS CLAIMED BY HIS ONLY LIVING RELATIVE, A DISTANT COUSIN...

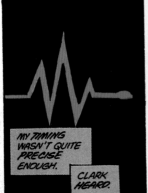

MY *TIMING* WASN'T QUITE PRECISE ENOUGH.

CLARK *HEARD.*

THAT WAS THE FIRST THING ROBIN *TOLD ME* --

--WHEN SHE *DUG ME UP.*

NOT THAT IT *MATTERED.* HE'D HAVE GUESSED SOONER OR LATER.

HE KNOWS HOW *GOOD* I AM WITH *CHEMICALS.*

I WAS *COUNTING* ON WHAT *OLIVER* SAID. AND WITH A -- *WINK* --

--CLARK PROVED OLIVER *RIGHT.*

WITH ACKNOWLEDGMENTS
TO THE WORKS OF

BILL FINGER

DAVE FLEISCHER

MAX FLEISCHER

JERRY ROBINSON

JOE SHUSTER

JERRY SIEGEL

DICK SPRANG

BATMAN CREATED BY
BOB KANE

GALLERY

THE ORIGINAL COVERS

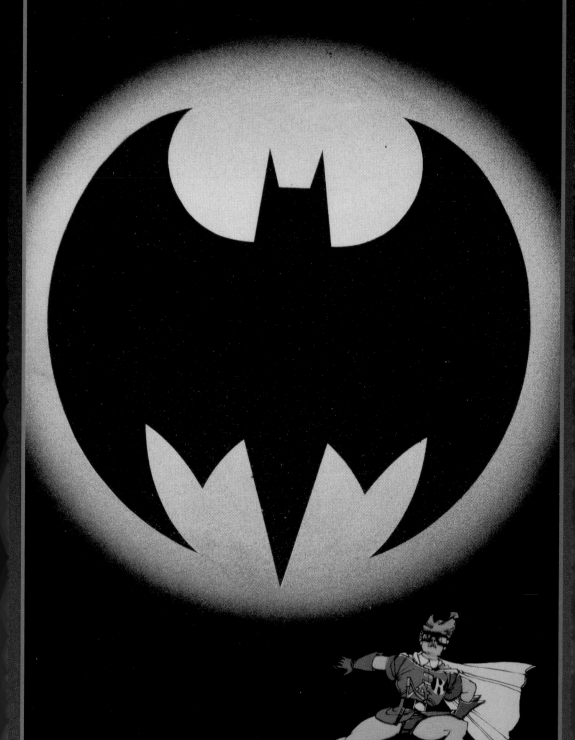

BOOK TWO

HUNT THE DARK KNIGHT

THE DARK KNIGHT FALLS

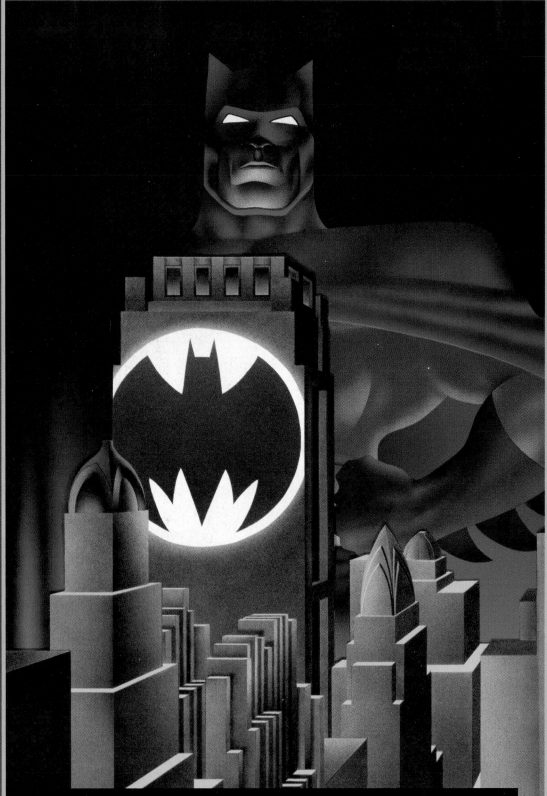

WARNER BOOKS

Book One cover used for DC edition

THE FIRST 48-PAGE CHAPTER OF
THE DARK KNIGHT RETURNS WAS DONE IN A
FULL SCRIPT VERSION (ART DESCRIPTIONS, PANEL-BY-PANEL
PAGE BREAKDOWNS, FINISHED CAPTIONS AND DIALOGUE).
SUBSEQUENT CHAPTERS, AS DEADLINE PRESSURES INCREASED
AND THE CREATIVE PROCESS BECAME MORE CONFIDENT, WERE
DONE FROM DETAILED PLOTS SUCH AS THE ONE THAT
FOLLOWS, WITH DIALOGUE AND CAPTIONS WORKED OUT AT
THE ROUGH PENCIL STAGE AND WITH CHANGES UP UNTIL THE
FINAL LETTERING WAS DONE (AND OCCASIONALLY AFTER
THAT). ALL OF THESE GIVE INSIGHT INTO THE DEVELOPMENTS
AND DECISIONS IN BRINGING A MAJOR WORK TO FRUITION.

THE PLOT FOR THE LAST CHAPTER,
THE DARK KNIGHT FALLS, IS PARTICULARLY
INTERESTING FOR THE WAY IT BUILDS TO A SUBTLY
DIFFERENT AND DARKER ENDING. THE CHANGES THAT BECAME
THE PUBLISHED VERSION GAVE US TRUER AND MORE
EMOTIONALLY SATISFYING VERSIONS OF BOTH BATMAN AND
SUPERMAN AND THE CLIMAX IN GENERAL. STILL, THERE IS
GREAT FASCINATION IN SEEING BATMAN FALL BY HIS OWN
HAND RATHER THAN BATTLING SUPERMAN, IN OBSERVING
THAT THERE IS NO ROLE PROVIDED FOR GREEN ARROW
(A CREEPY GOVERNMENT AGENT FULFILLS A SIMILAR
FUNCTION IN A MUCH MORE CYNICAL WAY), AND IN
ADMIRING THE SWITCH FROM THE FINAL IMAGE SUGGESTED
HERE TO THE ONE ULTIMATELY USED.

THE DARK KNIGHT FALLS

A DC GRAPHIC NOVEL
A STORY FOR 46 PAGES

BY FRANK MILLER
12/26/85

PUT TOGETHER POLITICAL FACTS
—KNOWLEDGE OF BOMB IS LEAD-IN
TO BATS' POLITICAL AWARENESS...

ACT 1
[PP 1–12]

Commissioner Yindel and a squad of armed cops pilot boats into the tunnel of love, looking for Batman and the Joker. Both ends of the tunnel are blocked, surrounded by cop cars and dozens of cops. In the middle of the tunnel, a cop calls out to Yindel. He's found the Joker's corpse. In the darkness, Yindel and her men converge on the corpse—but the cop who called out has vanished.

On the roller coaster, Robin sits, still in shock. She is struck by a brilliant arc light. A huge voice booms, ordering her not to move. It's from a police helicopter, hovering by the moving roller coaster, trying to track it with the arc light. Robin does not respond or react. She's crying, shivering, and stunned. A voice crackles over her wrist communicator. Robin, it says, I need you. Robin shakes herself, for the first time aware of her situation. As the helicopter banks and turns, trying to keep her in sight, Robin tumbles from the coaster to a lower track, swings herself under it, invisible to the copter. She pulls a small device from her glove, the same device she used to summon the Wing, earlier. She expertly presses buttons on the device. I need firepower, she thinks. It'll take ten minutes to get here. She looks down. Armed cops are climbing the coasters toward her. She doesn't have ten minutes.

In the tunnel, Yindel and her men shine searchlights across the water, looking for Batman, with orders to shoot. Yindel's light catches the shape of a man, coming up from the water. The cop in the boat with Yindel aims his rifle. Yindel shoves his gun down as he fires. The cop who found the Joker is the man who surfaced. He's unconscious.

Two of the cops bring their boat up next to the Joker's corpse. They move to pull him onto the boat. As soon as they move the corpse, something explodes from behind the Joker. Tear gas fills the tunnel. He rigged the body, says Yindel, donning a small gas mask. Keep those lights shining. He can't breathe underwater.

Underwater, wearing a small device in this mouth, Batman places a device on the underside of Yindel's boat. Blood drifts from him.

Outside the tunnel, cops see tear gas drift out of the tunnel. The sound of explosions erupts from the tunnel. The cops charge in.

Inside the tunnel, the cops find Yindel and her men in the water, surrounded by fragments of their boats. The water is only waist deep, though, and the cops wade, guns out, in military formation. The gas clears. One cop, nervous, jumps in terror as something wet splatters on the top of his helmet. He looks up. A second drop of blood strikes his visor. He gestures upward to a cop near him, who shines a spotlight upward, at Batman, who clings to the tunnel roof. Batman dives, into the water, as the cops open fire. He begins fighting the cops, hand to hand. Have to get to the mouth of the tunnel, he thinks. Then I'm counting on Robin.

On the roller coaster, the cops close in on Robin, who climbs up the tracks. One cop gets her in his sights. Another cop stops him from firing. No guns, he says. Not with the kid. Yindel's orders. The cops are about to reach Robin as she leaps from one track to another, then bounds into space, flipping, landing on the coaster as it begins its descent. The coaster roars on, along a curve, then rockets down the track, right at the cops. The cops jump to either side, dodging the coaster. The police copter tracks Robin, staying close. Suddenly the Batcopter appears in the night sky. As Robin shouts an order, the Batcopter flies in, between tracks, to hover directly over the coaster. Robin grabs a lowered wheel, is lifted away, as the police copter, knocked sideways by the wind created by the larger Batcopter, banks, trying to stay aloft.

Cops pile on Batman as he reaches the mouth of the tunnel. Suddenly, machine gun fire rips across the water. The cops fall away as Batman staggers out of the tunnel and collapses. Robin dives from the Batcopter. As bullets strike the water around her, she grabs Batman's arm, struggles to lift him.

Throughout all of this, TV coverage continues, with Hernando Hernandez and Lola Chong. Batman and Robin escape the police. Murder is added to the charges against the Batman.

In a 7–Eleven, somewhere in Gotham City, an off-duty police detective opens a refrigerator cabinet and reaches in for a six-pack of beer. He hears a commotion from the front of the store, and peers down an aisle to see four hoods harassing the store's clerk, waving pistols, knocking over cans and bottles, and demanding the clerk empty the cash register. The detective moves down the aisle, slowly, drawing his gun. He comes up behind the hoods, tells them not to move. A fifth hood, out of sight until now, raises his pistol to the detective's temple and giggles.

Outside the store, a sixth hood, waiting in the would-be getaway car, recoils at the sound of a gunshot, curses, and shifts the car to drive, as three men on motorcycles pull into the parking lot. The hood in the car looks in terror at the motorcycles, whose riders are as yet silhouetted by streetlight, their features indistinguishable. The hood floors the accelerator, and the car roars across the lot. One of the bikers gestures. Another lights a Molotov cocktail, and throws it into the passing car. The car catches fire. The hood, aflame, tumbles out, onto the parking lot. He looks up. A sawed-off shotgun barrel presses to his face. The shotgun blast is lost in the roar of the car exploding.

Inside the store, the hoods wheel, lit by the flame of the explosion. They freeze, not knowing what to do. Suddenly, the glass front of the shop explodes inward, from shotgun blasts.

Silhouetted by the flame, three Sons of the Batman step forward, to stand framed by broken glass, their shotguns held casually by their sides. They wait until the hoods in the store raise their pistols to fire. They blow the hoods apart with shotgun blasts.

The clerk is left, in the mess of blood, produce, and bodies, screaming in horror. Add SOB tape—"Let Gotham criminals beware."

Taped commentary by the late Dr. Bartholomew Wolper leads into commentary by Wolper's widow, who claims that Batman's murder of the Joker should be enough to link Batman to the actions of the Sons of the Batman.

Commentary continues, as the governor and mayor are briefly interviewed. They are no longer sidestepping the issue. It has become a political necessity to attack the Batman. People on the street are interviewed, as well. Batman has apparently few supporters. The only supporter quoted is a survivalist lunatic.

At Gotham's jail, Yindel is harassed by an attorney as she passes cells filled with captured Mutants. The attorney is protesting the overcrowded conditions. Yindel is wondering what she's going to do with them. The Mutants are angry, confused. Their gang is dead. Members of it are now the Sons of the Batman. They don't know what to do with themselves.

In the Batcave, Robin sits nervously outside a closed door. The door opens, and Alfred steps out, exhausted, wearing a surgical gown, his arms bloody to the elbow. He'll make it, asks Robin. He'll live, says Alfred.

TV news coverage resumes, with the president announcing that Soviet forces have withdrawn from Corto Maltese.

Clark Kent rides in a jeep across the burned-out remains of Corto Maltese. He's weary, tired, but can't help listening to news broadcasts. He hears about the Joker's apparent murder. Bruce, he thinks. You're finished. Sitting beside Clark is an Air Force general, who talks triumphantly about the victory. Clark looks up, then, skyward, alarmed. He silences the general, and listens.

A Soviet nuclear warhead roars through the sky.

The general, startled, looks at the seat next to him. Clark's clothes collapse, empty.

An advisor wakes the President, in the middle of the night, to inform him that the Soviets have launched a nuclear missile. The missile will explode over Corto Maltese in fifteen minutes. Get me my Pepto, says the President. And call the usual gang together.

A computer screen lights, showing the missile as a blip approaching Corto. General Lockheed screams at the President. This is an act of war, he says. Give the word. Not just yet, says the President. Let's see what our own little deterrent can do.

Superman tackles the rocket, two minutes from detonation. Slowly, he pushes, veering its course. You laughed at them, Bruce, he thinks. They can make this and you laugh at them. Superman counts the number of lives who will be lost at Corto if he fails, and keeps pushing.

Superman and the missile fly over a mountain range. He counts the victims again, including every animal and plant. He strains, shifts the course of the missile again. He and the missile fly over open desert. The count of victims now is twelve snakes and three dozen scorpions. Superman describes desert life, too, in detail—frogs that hybernate underground, hyenas, etc. He settles for that. He lets go of the rocket, and flies away from it, as fast as he can.

The President addresses the nation.

Don't worry, he says. It's not World War III. We're still America, he says, smiling. And I'm still President. Suddenly, the TV screen goes blank.

Superman is caught in the flash as the warhead detonates.

Robin and Alfred sit, in Wayne Manor. Bruce is in a hospital-style bed, unconscious, surrounded by monitors that show his vital signs. Robin watches the cardiogram, fixed on it, as Alfred tries to convince her to eat. Robin recoils, horrified, as the cardiogram goes flat, then stops. Then she realizes the room is dark, as well. A blackout, she says. Alfred, at the window, tells her that it must be a huge blackout. Gotham City is dark. How am I getting home, asks Robin. It must be late. Alfred pulls his watch from his pocket. The watch has stopped.

Bruce's eyes open. Clark, he thinks. You idiot. You let them do it. I always knew you would.

Superman is tossed like a burning ragdoll in the nuclear fireball. The desert vanishes in an enormous mushroom cloud.

Using SOBs is Robin's idea—+ she makes it work.

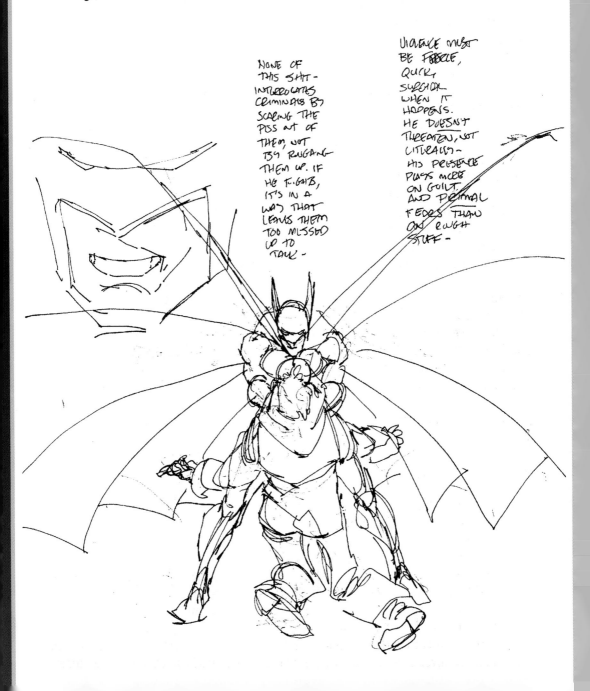

ACT II
[PP 13-24]

A commercial jet flies over the black silhouette of Gotham City. The pilot screams into a dead microphone. A stewardess screams to the pilot that the passengers are panicking. The jet falls through the night sky, collides with a skyscraper. Flames burst from the skyscraper. Glass, stone, then the plane itself, now aflame, fall toward the street, into a crowded intersection of stalled cars. The cars explode, one by one, as their gas tanks ignite. A lone traffic cop tries to maintain order amid the explosions and screaming crowd. He fires a shot into the air. A man tackles him, strikes him unconscious, and steals his pistol. It's the end of the world, the man says. It's every man for himself. And I've got a gun.

At Wayne Manor, Robin dutifully helps Bruce walk down a long corridor. Get the costume, Bruce says to Alfred, ignoring Alfred's protests. Down this way, Bruce says to Robin. To the stables.

In a crowded subway train, deep underground, people wait, silent, terrified, wondering if they are to be survivors of a holocaust. A priest prays aloud.

The window to a Gotham gun shop explodes inward. A frightened mob enters the store, grabs weapons and ammunition.

Fire spreads from the site of the airplane crash, across Gotham's West Side. James Gordon, on the street, drops a bag of groceries as he sees the pandemonium around him. He looks up to see his own building in flames. Sarah, he screams, then calms himself. He can't afford to think of Sarah. He grabs a man near him, who's running, holding a crowbar. The man raises the crowbar to strike Gordon. Gordon shoves his magnum into the man's face, tells the man to do what he's told. Gordon starts shouting orders to the people around him, and, hearing the authority in his voice, people respond. A fire hydrant is smashed open. Containers are found, garbage cans, milk cartons, all kinds, and a bucket brigade forms. The crowd, no longer panicking, gets to work against the fire. Gordon coughs, engulfed in smoke, and continues his orders.

At the dump, across the river from Gotham, the Sons of the Batman, holding torches, argue. There are two dozen of them, and they can't agree on what to do. Their commander screams that this is their chance to take power, to rape Gotham, spread fires—to purge Gotham.

Something explodes in their midst, tossing them and the dump's wreckage in all directions. They rise, guns out, ready for combat, as two figures approach on horseback. Against Gotham's flaming silhouette, Batman appears, riding a black stallion. Robin follows, leading horses. There will be no looting, commands Batman. Tonight we are the law. Tonight, I am the law. The commander points his shotgun at Batman. The man next to him shoots the commander dead. We await your orders, leader, he says to Batman. Come with me, says Batman. We need more men.

In the subway train, a yuppie accountant tells the priest to shut up, starts demanding they kick some people off the train. He stops demanding, as a switchblade appears at his throat. A black man, who looks every inch the urban criminal, big radio and all, tells the yuppie to shut up. Keep praying, the black man says to the priest. You can stop when my radio starts working again.

On Gotham's flaming West Side, Gordon's bucket brigade fights the fire, as burn victims are dragged from the buildings. Two nurses, at the scene, with no equipment,

try to help the burn victims, unable to do more than cover them and feed them booze from a nearby liquor store. Gordon, his face a mask of pain, pauses for a moment to check his pulse, Gordon: If I die now, I'm—no use to anybody. then turns as he hears Sarah's voice. She appears as a silhouette in the doorway to their building, backlit by flame. She runs toward him, just clearing the doorway as, behind her, a gas main ignites. She's thrown forward, to Gordon, on fire. He wraps his trenchcoat around her, screaming her name again and again.

In the jail, the imprisoned Mutants scream and thrash. They smell smoke. The fire has continued to spread, and flames leap from a nearby building to the jailhouse. Yindel shouts orders to her frightened men. Merkel tells her there's no way to save the jailhouse. She pauses for a moment, looks over the Mutants. She sees a young one burst into tears. Let them go, she says.

The Mutants spill from the jail into the street, yelping and hungry for blood. Tonight is our night, says one. Let's party. One picks up a piece of burning wood, raises it high above his head. The fiery end of the wood is blasted by shotgun fire.

Batman, Robin, and the Sons of the Batman ride up on horses. Two dozen shotguns are aimed at the cornered Mutants. Swear allegiance to me, says Batman, or die. The Mutants pause, confused. Then, behind them, appears Yindel and several cops, guns drawn. Batman eyes them. It won't end tonight, he declares. The nightmare has only begun. The power will return by morning. But there will be no morning. The bomb, he says, furious, the bomb exploded over a desert. That desert is now in the sky, spreading across the hemisphere. It will blacken the sky over Gotham. It will blot out the sun—and the moon. As he speaks, the moon is obscured by black clouds. The shadow crawls across the frightened Mutants. One by one, they remove their visors. Yindel steps back, ordering her men to do the same. Merkel asks her why. He's too big, she says, distantly. Kneel, says Batman. Swear. The Mutants fall to their knees. One of the Sons of the Batman fires his shotgun into the air. Gotham City belongs to the Batman, he says.

In the desert, now a sheet of blackened glass, a tank-like vehicle, powered by hydraulics, moves through sheets of flame. The sky above is black. Hoses pop from the vehicle, spraying foam, quenching the fire on a small patch of glass. Men emerge, heavily armored, with large devices that resemble stethoscopes. They attach the devices to the floor. Through hand gestures they indicate that there is no sign of Agent Kent.

They're about to board their vehicle when they are knocked to their feet by a deep rumble that shakes the earth. The glass cracks, and a blackened, almost skeletal figure breaks through the crust. He looks like a zombie, his costume hanging from little more than bone. He looks up to the sky. There is no sun to power him. He rises to his feet, shaky, and keeps rising, slowly, from the earth. He must find the sun, he thinks, rising through atomic flames into the sky.

In Gotham, Gordon hovers over Sarah, talking hysterically to her, feeding her whiskey. She's badly burned, but she'll live. He looks up, to see black faces, awaiting orders, as building after building bursts into flame. Gordon lifts Sarah, still wrapped in his coat. We can't save the neighborhood, he says. Carry the wounded.

So many need me, thinks Clark, rising into the sky, toward the clouds. Enormous, unearthly lightning flashes, a magnetic storm caused by the disruption of the earth's magnetic field. Awkwardly, he tries to maneuver through it. He is struck by a lightning bolt. It doesn't tickle. He falls to earth, now hundreds of miles from the desert. He is unconscious.

In Gotham, the mob who robbed the gun shop breaks into a grocery store. An armed guard points his pistol and tells them to stop. Someone in the mob fires a rifle, and the guard falls dead, crashing into a shelf of canned food. The canned stuff, screams somebody in the mob, and they begin filling grocery carts with cans. They're exiting the store when they hear the sound of horses approaching.

Two Sons of the Batman, on horseback, lead a dozen armed Mutants to the grocery stores. Drop your weapons, says an SOB. And drop the food. One of the mob raises a pistol. The SOB blows him apart with a shotgun blast. To the west side, says the SOB to the mob. Get to work on the fires. We speak for the Batman.

What seems to be a meteor strikes a South American jungle, making the ground shudder and smashing through foliage. Clark lies in a crater, dying. He crawls, slowly, to the edge of the crater. He can't reach the sun. But the sun's power is held on earth. Photosynthesis, he thinks. So many need me. He reaches the edge of the crater, touches a patch of earth, then a beautiful jungle flower. The flower wilts, and dies. Then, spreading outward from Clark, the jungle dies, for miles around. Clark rises, looking like a man again, severely depowered, but Superman again. He rises into the air. The world is screaming to him.

Batman gives orders to SOBs, like a general commanding troops, giving each group of Mutants and SOBS different neighborhoods to protect. He sags, momentarily, in his saddle, then continues. Robin looks at him.

An airplane falls from the sky toward Rio. Superman flies beneath it, struggles with its weight. He can't keep it aloft, but uses his body to cushion its landing. He rises from beneath its crumpled front end, shakes himself, and leaps skyward.

In the subway train, the priest prays, then stops as he hears the crackle of a radio.

ACT III
[PP 25-36]

Gotham City squats beneath a black layer of clouds. The city's lights are on. Snow falls.

On TV, the Vice President addresses the nation. The President is dead, he says grimly. As a precaution, the President was flown high above the earth in Air Force One. Air Force One fell from the sky like a rock when all electrical activity ceased on the hemisphere. The bomb, he continues, was of a kind that the U.S. had not suspected existed—a Soviet creation called the Coldbringer, designed to cause maximum ecological damage. So, while its immediate effects were what experts expected, the magnetic pulse it produced, and the dirt and soot it spread, were comparable to that of a much larger nuclear strike. The Soviets wished to teach us a lesson, says the Vice President. But, to everyone's surprise, they did not take advantage of the blackout, which paralyzed U.S. nuclear capability, by following through with a total attack. We taught them a lesson, though, once the lights came on. We blew Cuba from the face of the earth.

Days pass. Superman and Batman work nonstop to maintain order. The Vice President declares a state of stabilized emergency.

Commissioner Yindel orders the Sons of the Batman arrested, but none are to be found, thanks to Batman's continued leadership. The warrant for murder against the Batman sparks cautious discussion about costumed individuals who set themselves apart from the rest of humanity.

A huge locomotive pulls into Gotham Central Station. From it steps Clark Kent. He buys a newspaper, reads an editorial complaining, in folksy terms, about so-called heroes who think they're better than everybody else. Something ought to be done, it says. Something is going to be done, thinks Clark, folding the newspaper. You crossed over the line, Bruce. I'm bringing you in. But first, I'm taking care of your fan club.

A truck, carrying desperately needed medical supplies, stops on a Gotham avenue at the scene of an apparent accident. A sedan rests upside down on the icy street. Next to it, a woman lies on her back. Her belly is swelled, as if she's pregnant. A man leans over her, desperate. As the truck stops, the man turns, declaring that this is his wife, that despite the ban on cars, he was rushing her to the hospital to have a baby when the car overturned. In the truck, the driver tells the guard next to him to check it out. The guard balks, says that they aren't allowed to stop for anything, since several medical shipments have been robbed. The driver insists. We're still human, for Christ's sake, he says. Cautiously, the guard steps from the truck, his hand on his holstered pistol. From a snowbank pops a man, wearing a ski mask, pointing a submachine gun at the guard. The guard curses, and raises his hands. The woman rises, leering, and pulls a pistol from her false stomach. Out of the truck, she says, and the driver complies. What the hell, she says, cocking her pistol. Let's kill them. Wait a minute, says the man. You hear horses?

Three Sons of the Batman ride up, carrying shotguns. They aim them. The thieves pivot, about to open fire. Suddenly, a huge wind rips down the avenue, an icy blizzard that tosses the SOBs from their horses and sends the thieves skittering along the icy street. Fiercer it blows. The snow is blinding white. After a few moments it dies down, leaving the guard and driver with their truck, alone on the avenue.

TV news reveals that SOBs are appearing at Gotham Jail in alarming numbers, trussed up, helpless, but refusing to explain who or what brought them in. An SOB lieutenant makes a brief statement: Our leader will come for us.

Establish Robin as reason Bats stays alive.

Batman and Robin ride horses down another icy street, somewhere in Gotham. Robin wears earmuffs, and tights, in addition to her costume. Batman wears a chest-plate, one he designed, that electronically monitors his vital signs and keeps them stable. He's not healing as quickly as he expected. He watches Robin, amazed at how quickly she is learning to ride. He smiles as she goads the horse into leaping a high snowbank. She's a miracle, he thinks.

His own horse rears, abruptly, as a blast of heat strikes the street in front of him. He topples from the horse. Ice explodes on the street. There is a blast of steam. When it clears, a message is left, burned into the street, a single word: WHERE? Very softly, Batman says, Crime Alley. Robin helps him rise. What does this mean, she asks. He touches her cheek. It means you're fired, he says gently. He rides off. She follows.

TV news reports that the city's jail is overflowing with SOBs, far worse than it was with the Mutants earlier. It's obvious that the SOBs have grown, from a couple of dozen to an army. Yindel requests help from nearby prisons, just to find a place for all of them. Her request is refused. Alone in her office, Yindel wonders what she can do with them—and how long she can hold them.

At Wayne Manor, Batman, Robin, and Alfred stand in the Batcave. Batman is partially covered in black body armor. He snaps orders to Robin, telling her what her part is in the coming fight. He turns to Alfred, holds him by the shoulders. It's time, he says, old friend. You know what to do. Alfred nods solemnly. Batman and Robin work on arming a series of bombs as Alfred walks off.

TV reports that Crime Alley is evacuated by the National Guard, and cordoned off, with no explanation.

In her TV office, Lola Chong explodes at her superiors. She tells them that they and everyone in the media knows who brought the SOBs in, and that this evacuation may be the prelude to the story of the decade. She wants to investigate it, and broadcast it, FCC regulations be damned. Her superiors get nervous. She threatens to quit.

At Wayne Manor, alone, Alfred carefully polishes the Wayne family crest.

A cold wind blows down Crime Alley. A very cold wind.

A blip appears on a radar screen. Lit by the screen, Robin whispers into a microphone. I think he's here, she says. She listens to an earphone, presses a series of buttons.

A red boot touches the pavement.

The street erupts in a massive explosion. As it settles, a searchlight flashes down, probing the wrecked street. It strikes a figure, rising to his knees in the rubble. Superman looks up, to see a helicopter above him. He's in pain, and furious. His eyes turn red. Then, he turns away, violently. Superman: Innocents. They told me there weren't going to be any. The facade of a nearby building catches fire.

In the helicopter, Lola Chong excitedly orders the pilot to come in lower. We've found him, she says. Screw the FCC.

Superman dashes through an alleyway, not flying. He probes the neighborhood, his eyes glowing blue now, with X-ray vision. The X-rays ignite several hunter missiles, which fly toward him from all directions. He blasts three from the air, with heat. The fourth strikes him, smashing him through the front of a tenement as it explodes. The tenement collapses on him.

Lola Chong describes a battle of the gods in Crime Alley. She's interrupted as a fighter copter bearing Army insignia roars up beside hers, orders them to clear the area or be shot from the sky. Do as they say, says Lola. But fly low. As the News copter dips, turning from the area, Lola, carrying a portable camera and audio device, leaps from the copter to the street. Machine gun fire strikes the pavement behind her as she scrambles out of sight. She makes her way toward the collapsed tenement, taping, no longer broadcasting.

At Wayne Manor, Alfred stands before an enormous fireplace, with a roaring fire. He holds a large, leatherbound scrapbook, open, in his hands. It's open to an early page, featuring twenty-five-year-old clippings that announce the Batman's earliest assaults on crime in Gotham City. He runs his fingers gently over the clippings. He smiles and tosses the scrapbook into the fire.

Superman once again rises, his nose bloody now, his manner more calm—more irritated than angry. Machine gun fire rips across his chest, knocking him backward. The earth shudders. A nearby wall falls outward. The Batmobile rumbles into view, guns blazing.

Superman dodges the machine gun fire, as best he can. He smiles, says, isn't tonight a school night?

Inside the Batmobile, Robin talks into the microphone. Thought he couldn't see through lead, she says. He can hear through it, a voice tells her.

Superman cocks his head at the sound of Batman's voice, instantly pinpointing Batman's location two blocks away. As he turns to move in the direction of the voice, a load of napalm sprays across him. He bursts into flame. The Batmobile continues to rumble toward him. Setting his jaw, Superman, still aflame, faces off with it. He concentrates, but cannot summon his heat vision. A cannon pivots, aimed at him at point-blank range. He leaps to it, twists it upward, his teeth gritted with the effort. He lets go, falls under the Batmobile's track. The Batmobile rolls over him, then rises, and topples on its side. Superman grabs the hatch, rips it off. Inside squats Robin, terrified, her slingshot aimed. She watches as he rises into the sky.

From his vantage point, we see the street where Bruce's parents were murdered. Standing solemnly under the lamppost is Batman, dressed head to toe in gleaming black body armor. He watches Superman land, facing him ten feet away. Not good, thinks Batman. He can still fly.

Superman walks up to Batman. It's over, he says. Come along. Don't make me hurt you. Don't touch me, says Batman, holding a hand up. His other hand holds the lamp. Superman grabs the hand. His back arches, his hair stands on end, as a huge electrical charge rips through him. Batman sags against the lamp, holding fast to it and to Superman's hand. The lights dim in Gotham. Superman sags to his knees.

Lola steps into the street, filming and narrating.

In agony, Superman grabs Batman by the chestplate, pulls him from the post, slams him back into it. Batman punches Superman, his strength enormously amplified by the armor, and Superman falls on his back, astonished and enraged, now bleeding from the mouth. It's the sun, says Batman. Without it, you grow weaker by the minute. You could lose. Superman swings his fist. Batman ducks. The lamppost is bent in half by Superman's punch. Batman steps in, punches Superman in the solar plexus. You're a slob, Clark, he says. You've always been a slob. He kicks Superman in the throat. Superman falls, curled, coughing, on the street. Batman slaps a device on Superman's head, backs away as it explodes.

Lola is seized by government agents. They smash her camera and put her in handcuffs.

Superman is flat on the ground, still alive. Say uncle, says Batman. Superman struggles to rise. Batman kicks him in the face. Superman lies on his back. Batman turns, and walks away. Half a block from Superman, Batman stops, noticing that it is no longer snowing. No, he thinks. Oh, no. He looks skyward.

Sunlight creeps through the dark sky.

Sunlight strikes Superman. His wounds begin to heal. Batman turns to face him as he rises to one knee. Batman draws a huge pistol from a leg sheath and fires. An explosive bullet strikes Superman between the eyes. Superman punches the pavement. Batman topples to the street. Superman rises, walks toward him. The sky is red now, as if on fire. Batman fires again, the bullet exploding against Superman's chest— for tradition, thinks Batman. Superman seizes the gun, crushes it easily. Sadly, he says, Bruce, it's really over. Just listen to your heart. That portable hospital bed you're wearing doesn't make you invulnerable.

Nobody's invulnerable, says Batman, as green gas pours from his suit, enveloping both of them in a cloud. Superman falls back, coughing, horrified. It was tough to synthesize, says Batman. Took years. You see, I always knew I'd have to do something about you someday. Superman reels, takes a step backward. Batman chuckles, daunting Superman. He grabs him by the hair. Talk to Lois lately, says Batman.

Superman roars, in rage. Windows shatter. Batman is smashed into the air, into a brick wall, which gives way. Batman staggers to his feet. Superman leaps, tackling him, smashing through empty rooms. Wild with rage, he punches Batman, knocking his helmet off. Then he stops, and steps backward, seeing Bruce's face. Blood streams from Bruce's mouth and nose. Truce, says Clark. Your heart. Bruce collapses. His face is pale. His eyes are squinted in agony. He smiles crookedly, and passes out. His heart stops.

No, mutters Superman. You planned it this way. I won't let you get away with it. He grabs Bruce and lifts him as soldiers converge. Medic, he screams.

At Wayne Manor, Alfred carefully dusts a matched set of photographs of Thomas, Martha, and Bruce Wayne. He sets them neatly on a shelf. He opens a grand-father clock, and rearranges the weights. He walks from Wayne Manor, out to the moors, turns and faces the huge mansion. He stands, unsteadily, as the ground trembles. Wayne Manor shakes with the sound of underground explosions. It collapses in on itself, then falls in pieces into the earth, into the Batcave.

Alfred brushes a tear away, smiles, and falls dead in the grass.

ACT IV
[PP 37-47]

Soldiers converge on the damaged Batmobile, guns out. It lies on its side. The soldiers fall back as it rights itself, and roars forward, down the street. An army helicopter fires a rocket at it, to no effect. Another helicopter joins the scene. An intense Federal Agent, named Haggard, rides in the new copter. Track it, he orders. It'll take us to the son of a bitch's headquarters.

The Batmobile rumbles into a run-down, abandoned tenement. It smashes through a wall at full speed, and crashes down, through the rotted floor. Soldiers swarm the tenement, shining lights down into the tenement's basement. The Batmobile is gone. A wall of the basement is smashed through, revealing a huge unused water main.

Robin, inside the speeding Batmobile, punches a program and leans back in the seat, tense but unafraid. He won't die, she thinks. I won't even think about that. There's too much to do...

A fiery sky paints Gotham red. Looking stunned, Lola Chong appears on TV, announcing that Batman has been arrested by federal agents.

At an Army hospital, Haggard shows his identification to an armed guard, then enters a room, in which lies Bruce Wayne, plugged into all sorts of life support machinery. He lies still, eyes open, staring forward. Clark Kent leans by a window, intense. Haggard smiles at Clark, holds his hand out. Clark ignores the hand. He's stabilized, says Clark. You'll have to watch out for suicide attempts. When you question him, you are not to harm him in any way. Haggard's smile is awkward. Kent, he says, you're needed in the Midwest. The crop failure's causing serious trouble. It's practically civil war. Clark grimaces. It's much worse than you told me, he says. And I let you do it. Hey, says Haggard, it was the Russians, remember? Clark leaves.

Alone with Bruce, Haggard grows more confident. You're not going to trial, he says. Or to jail. As a matter of fact, you'll probably get your very own Agency. Once we're done with the questioning, of course. We've got a lot to learn from you. Bruce looks at Haggard and grins, amused. We're going to be great friends, says Haggard.

On TV, Lola Chong announces that Federal sources have divulged that Batman is Bruce Wayne—and is in critical condition. Doctors are not hopeful. In a related story, Wayne Manor has been destroyed. An enormous cave has been discovered beneath the site of Wayne Manor, apparently the Batman's base of operations. However, whatever secrets it might have revealed have been lost, burned to ashes. The cave's only entrance has been sealed by authorities.

The Batmobile rumbles out of an abandoned subway station. Robin presses a button on its controls. An inner lid seals the cab, making it airtight. She drives it into the river. It rumbles along the river bed. A flashing signal appears on the screen. Robin frowns. I'm running late, she thinks.

A nurse checks Bruce's vital signs, then lifts his head, fluffs up his pillow, and sets his head back down. Bruce smiles at her, warmly. She kisses his forehead. A lot of us love you, she says, and leaves the room.

Alone, Bruce becomes alert. His face is eager. He sits up in bed, and pulls a tube from his arm. His arm begins to bleed. Ignoring it, he gouges his forearm with the needle from the tube, cutting through his flesh. It's very painful, and bloody, but he looks like he's enjoying it. He digs into his arm with his fingers, extracts a small capsule. He puts it in his mouth and bites. He shudders, from head to foot. He arches his back. His vital signs go wild, then stop. His cardiogram becomes a straight red line.

On TV, it is reported that Bruce Wayne died in surgery. A surgeon is interviewed, briefly.

Carrying a freight car loaded with grain, Superman turns, in horror.

Bruce Wayne lies on a slab in the hospital morgue. Haggard screams at agents, points at the corpse. Bruce is naked; there are no marks of surgery on him. An agent, looking harassed, points at a cut on Bruce's forearm. Jesus, he says to Haggard. We checked him from head to toe. We checked his teeth, and every orifice in his body. He had the cyanide hidden under his goddamn skin. You want an autopsy, asks a bored attendant. Forget it, says Haggard. Son of a bitch is no use to us now.

At Gotham Jail, Commissioner Yindel walks past cells filled with SOBs, who sit, calmly, silently. Yindel is suspicious, and nervous.

On TV, it is announced that the IRS, investigating the Wayne Estate, has found every part of Wayne Enterprises has self-destructed, every stock has been sold, every penny of the Wayne fortune has ceased to exist. Bruce Wayne died broke, says the anchorman.

The Batmobile rises from the river, drives to the mudhole where Batman fought the Mutant leader in DARK KNIGHT TRIUMPHANT. Robin climbs from the mudhole as the Batmobile sinks, slowly, into the mud. She climbs to the pipe, and crawls inside.

At Gotham Jail, one SOB whispers to another. Bitch is late, he says. The cell door opens. You coming or what, a voice says.

On TV, it is reported that the SOBs vanished from their cells. Despite an intensive search, no sign of them has been found.

Bruce Wayne is buried, with a surprising crowd in attendance. The funeral is broadcast on TV. Featured are James Gordon, overcome with grief, Clark Kent, tight-lipped, looking somewhat older, Ellen Yindel, strangely respectful, and Selina Kyle, inarticulate with rage. The crowd hangs on long after the service, finally thinning, to Selina, Clark, Gordon, and Carrie Kelley, who does her best to look sad. The sun is rising as Selina collapses across Bruce's grave. Gordon pulls her away, takes her to his car. Clark and Carrie stand together by the grave. Clark pats Carrie on the shoulder, and turns to walk away, then stops, and turns back, staring at the fresh earth, startled. Clark breaks into a painful grin. Carrie stares at him, frightened. Clark gives Carrie a classic Superman wink, and walks off.

Carrie stands alone at the grave for a few seconds. Then she grabs a shovel.

Night falls on Gotham City. TV news reviews the international situation. Limited Nuclear War is now a reality, and tensions continue to mount. Every nation on earth is equipped with nuclear weapons, and a fearsome Terrorist Alliance is likewise equipped.

The remains of Wayne Manor seem tiny on the floor of the Batcave. The ashes that were once Batman's arsenal coat a patch of the cave floor. But the cave itself is enormous beyond belief. It stretches back, and down into the earth, for miles. Far down, far from what was once Batman's headquarters, a hundred torches burn.

Lit by the torches, on a throne made of living oak, sits the Batman. Robin stands at his side. Behind them, in military formation, holding the torches, stand the Sons of the Batman.

Bruce Wayne is dead. The Dark Knight lives.
And he has learned that there is more wrong with the world than crime.

-30-

ALSO BY FRANK MILLER:

BATMAN: THE DARK KNIGHT STRIKES AGAIN

(W) Miller (A) Miller/Varley

The sequel to Frank Miller's classic BATMAN: THE DARK KNIGHT RETURNS finds a seemingly perfect world — but Batman knows better. He's about to take on the corruption bubbling beneath the surface, and he's recruited the World's Greatest Heroes to help him!

BATMAN: YEAR ONE

(W) Miller (A) Mazzucchelli (C) Lewis

Frank Miller's dramatic look at Batman's first year of crimefighting is the master storyteller at his finest. The origin of Gotham City's Dark Knight, who he is, and how he came to be is accentuated by David Mazzucchelli's moody, distinctive artwork.

RONIN

(W/A) Miller (C) Varley

In this collection of Miller's classic 6-issue miniseries (which Miller describes as a "super-hero, science fiction, samurai drama, urban nightmare, gothic romance"), a 13th-century warrior is reborn in the 21st century to battle a demonic foe.

MORE EXCITING COLLECTIONS FROM TITAN BOOKS!

BATMAN: ARKHAM ASYLUM

(W) G. Morrison (A) McKean

BATMAN: THE LONG HALLOWEEN

(W) Loeb (A) Sale

BIZARRO COMICS

(W/A) Various

CRISIS ON INFINITE EARTHS

(W) Wolfman (A) Pérez/Ordway/Giordano

GREEN ARROW: QUIVER

(W) K. Smith (A) Hester/Parks

JLA: EARTH 2

(W) G. Morrison (A) Quitely

KINGDOM COME

(W) Waid (A) A. Ross

WATCHMEN

(W) A. Moore (A) Gibbons